FODOR'S TRAVEL GUIDES

are compiled, researched, and edited by an international team of travel writers, field correspondents, and editors. The series, which now almost covers the globe, was founded by Eugene Fodor in 1936.

OFFICES
New York & London

Fodor's Chesapeake:

Editor: James Louttit
Area Coordinator: Editorial Ink, Ltd.
Contributing Editors: Edgar and Patricia Cheatham, James Day, Steve Doherty, Eleanor Ely, Rodney N. Smith
Research: Jacqueline Russell
Maps: Burmar Technical Corp.
Drawings: Amy Harold

FODOR'S®
CHESAPEAKE

FODOR'S TRAVEL GUIDES
New York & London

Parts of this book also appear in *Fodor's Virginia*

The following Fodor's Guides are current; most are also available in a British
edition published by Hodder & Stoughton.

Country and Area Guides

Australia, New Zealand
  & The South Pacific
Austria
Bahamas
Belgium & Luxembourg
Bermuda
Brazil
Canada
Canada's Maritime
  Provinces
Caribbean
Central America
Eastern Europe
Egypt
Europe
France
Germany
Great Britain
Greece
Holland
India, Nepal &
  Sri Lanka
Ireland
Israel
Italy
Japan
Jordan & The Holy Land
Kenya
Korea
Mexico
North Africa
People's Republic of
  China
Portugal
Scandanavia
Scotland
South America
Southeast Asia

Soviet Union
Spain
Switzerland
Turkey
Yugoslavia

City Guides

Amsterdam
Beijing, Guangzhou,
  Shanghai
Boston
Chicago
Dallas–Fort Worth
Greater Miami & The
  Gold Coast
Hong Kong
Houston
Lisbon
London
Los Angeles
Madrid
Mexico City &
  Acapulco
Munich
New Orleans
New York City
Paris
Philadelphia
Rome
San Diego
San Francisco
Stockholm, Copenhagen,
  Oslo, Helsinki &
  Reykjavik
Sydney
Tokyo
Toronto
Vienna
Washington, D.C.

U.S.A. Guides

Alaska
Arizona
California
Cape Cod
Colorado
Far West
Florida
Hawaii
New England
New Mexico
Pacific North Coast
South
Texas
U.S.A.

Budget Travel

American Cities (30)
Britain
Canada
Caribbean
Europe
France
Germany
Hawaii
Italy
Japan
London
Mexico
Spain

Fun Guides

Acapulco
Bahamas
London
Montreal
Puerto Rico
San Francisco
St. Martin/Sint Maarten
Waikiki

MANUFACTURED IN THE UNITED STATES OF AMERICA
10 9 8 7 6 5 4 3 2 1

CONTENTS

Map of Chesapeake Bay   vii

Foreword   xi

Introduction   1

FACTS AT YOUR FINGERTIPS

Boats and Boating, 11; When to Go, 11; Planning Your Trip, 12; Tourist Information, 13; Hints for Motorists, 14; On the Road in Maryland, 14; On the Road in Virginia, 14; Tips for British Visitors, 15; Tips for Disabled Travelers, 15; Time Zone and Area Codes, 16; Recommended Reading, 16; What It Will Cost, 16; Senior Citizen Discounts, 18; Places to Stay, 18; Places to Eat, 20; Seasonal Events, 22; Recreational Activities, 26; Swimming, 26; Ferry Rides and Cruises, 27; Parks and Forests, 28; Canoeing, 29; Fishing, 29; Yacht Chartering, 30; Colonial Sites, 31

THE CHESAPEAKE

The Chesapeake—Maryland and Virginia's Watery
Vacationland   37

Maryland's Western Shore—Three Southern Counties—
Calvert, Charles, and St. Mary's   44

    Map of the Western Shore   46

    Practical Information for Calvert, Charles, and
    St. Mary's Counties   47

Annapolis   51

    Map of the Annapolis Area   52

    Exploring Annapolis   54

    Practical Information for Annapolis   55

Baltimore   59

    Map of Baltimore Area   60

    Practical Information for Baltimore   62

The Upper Bay   70

    Map of the Upper Bay   71

    Practical Information for the Upper Bay   73

Maryland's Eastern Shore	80
Map of the Eastern Shore	82
Practical Information for Maryland's Eastern Shore	84
Ocean City and Worcester County	94
Map of Worcester County	95
Practical Information for Ocean City and Worcester County	97
Virginia's Eastern Shore	103
Map of the Eastern Shore	104
Practical Information for Virginia's Eastern Shore	109
Norfolk and Virginia Beach	111
Map of Norfolk and Virginia Beach	113
Practical Information for Norfolk and Virginia Beach	114
Tidewater Virginia	124
Map of Tidewater Virginia	126
Map of Williamsburg, Jamestown, and Yorktown Area—Colonial National Historical Park	128
Exploring Williamsburg	127
Practical Information for Williamsburg	130
Exploring Jamestown	136
Practical Information for Jamestown	137
Exploring Yorktown	138
Practical Information for Yorktown	139
Exploring Hampton and Newport News	141
Practical Information for Hampton and Newport News	142
Exploring James River Plantations	144
Virginia's Northern Neck	146
Map of Virginia's Northern Neck	147
Practical Information for Virginia's Northern Neck	148
Index	153

MAP OF
CHESAPEAKE

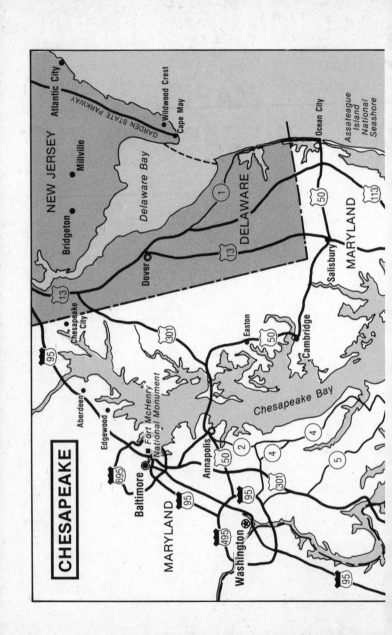

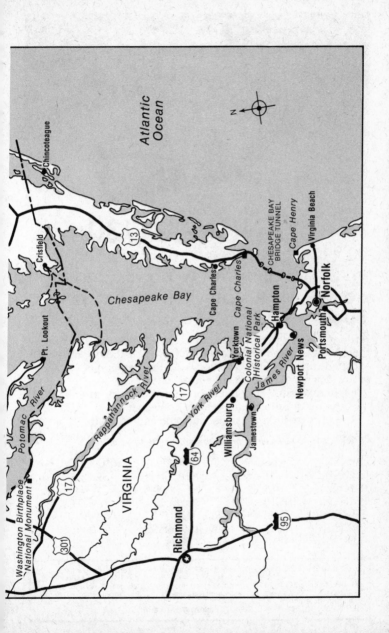

LANGUAGE/30

For the Business or Vacationing International Traveler

In 27 languages! A basic language course on 2 cassettes and a phrase book … Only $14.95 ea. + shipping

Nothing flatters people more than to hear visitors try to speak their language and LANGUAGE/30, used by thousands of satisfied travelers, gets you speaking the basics quickly and easily. Each LANGUAGE/30 course offers:

- approximately 1½ hours of guided practice in greetings, asking questions and general conversation
- special section on social customs and etiquette

Order yours today. Languages available: (New) POLISH

ARABIC	GREEK	KOREAN	SERBO-CROATIAN
CHINESE	HEBREW	NORWEGIAN	SPANISH
DANISH	HINDI	PERSIAN	SWAHILI
DUTCH	INDONESIAN	POLISH	SWEDISH
FINNISH	ITALIAN	PORTUGUESE	TAGALOG
FRENCH	TURKISH	VIETNAMESE	THAI
GERMAN	JAPANESE	RUSSIAN	

FOREWORD

Fodor's Chesapeake is a compact, rather personal touring guide to one of America's favorite vacation areas. We have not attempted to include each and every old church, burial mound, or quiet hamlet up and down the length of this great Bay—but we did *consider* them all, narrowing our final selections to those places that now appear in these pages. These, then, are a personal but experienced selection of Places to Eat and Stay and Things to See and Do that have been chosen to give you, the reader-traveler, the true flavor of this very special place—Chesapeake Bay.

Captain John Smith was delighted by the natural wonders of the Chesapeake when he toured the Bay in 1608. Smith, in time, committed his impressions to print—and thereby became the first Chesapeake travel writer. History and progress have added many "wonders" since Smith sailed these waters: Baltimore's rejuvenated Inner Harbor, picturesque Annapolis, two mighty Bay bridges, historic St. Mary's City, Colonial Williamsburg—the list could go on and on.

Chesapeake Bay is a favorite touring destination of the writers and editors who compiled these pages, and it is our hope that our efforts will enrich your enjoyment of Maryland and Virginia's Watery Vacationland. And finally, as we move on to more practical matters, we find ourselves musing: Would Captain Smith have approved?

The first section of *Fodor's Chesapeake*—Facts at Your Fingertips—is designed to help you plan your trip, providing general information on activities and attractions, as well as local facts—climate, transportation, and the like.

Next is an Introduction to the Chesapeake, its heritage and its history.

Following are detailed descriptions, ordered geographically, of the Bay by area. These have broad descriptions first and then Practical Information, which includes detailed descriptions, addresses, phone numbers and so forth for accommodations, restaurants, museums, parks, historical sites, and more.

The selections and comments in *Fodor's Chesapeake* are based on personal experiences. Change can and will occur around the Chesapeake while we are on press and in the year this edition will be on sale. We sincerely welcome letters from our readers about these changes, or from those whose opinions differ from ours. We will revise our entries for future editions when the facts warrant it.

Send your letter to the Publisher at Fodor's Travel Guides, 2 Park Avenue, New York, NY 10016. Continental or British Commonwealth readers may prefer to write to Fodor's Travel Guides, 9–10 Market Place, London W1N 7AG, England.

CHESAPEAKE

INTRODUCTION TO THE
CHESAPEAKE BAY AREA

by
STEVE DOHERTY

Chesapeake Bay is a unique topographical feature of the U.S. East Coast. Two hundred miles long from north to south, it is the largest inland body of water on the Atlantic Coast. (Small-boat sailors will note that Long Island Sound, while impressive as a body of protected water, is only 150 miles long.) The Chesapeake runs north and south, roughly parallel to the Atlantic. It is actually an estuary flowing into the ocean and, by penetrating deep into the land interior, has had a vital role in the development of this mid-Atlantic region. Visualize how long it would have taken to develop the vast land area touching the Chesa-

1

peake if there had been no Bay and only rutted, muddy wagon roads for transportation.

It's hard to exaggerate the importance of the Bay as a Colonial "water highway" for freight, farm produce, mail, and passengers. The early American cities were East Coast ports, with easy access to the Atlantic. Among these were Charleston, South Carolina; Norfolk, Virginia; Baltimore, Maryland; New York City; and Boston, Massachusetts. Even Philadelphia, so pivotal in America's early history, was easily reached by any ship that proceeded up Delaware Bay until it became a river.

Norfolk, just inside the mouth of the Bay, was an obvious site for a city, and Baltimore has been a major seaport since colonial days, simply because the Chesapeake was navigable for 150 miles north of the ocean. But the Chesapeake's importance goes beyond that. Even locally it shaped the way this part of the nation developed.

At the lower (Virginia) end of this great bay, when that state was still an English colony in the early 1600s, its first settlement was at Jamestown, which was also the capital. Virginia's second capital was Williamsburg. Both were on the banks of the James River, within easy reach of the Bay. Even after the capital was moved to Richmond some centuries later, that city was still reachable via the James.

Further north, in Maryland, it's the same story. The Maryland colony was founded in 1634, 27 years after Jamestown. Its capital was later established at Annapolis, facing east on the Chesapeake. Not only were Norfolk, Williamsburg, Richmond, Annapolis, and Baltimore within easy sailing distance of each other and of all the small waterfront towns that lay between, but perhaps more important, each could easily reach the national capital at Washington, D.C. by proceeding up the Potomac River from the Bay. During the Civil War Abraham Lincoln sometimes used the Bay as a quick route to the front lines so he could have face-to-face conferences with his commanders. Once he departed the White House surreptitiously (so as not to alarm the capital's populace where Confederate forces were less than 100 miles away), proceeded down the Potomac to the Bay in a fast steamboat, ran south to the James River, and then up that river to General U. S. Grant's headquarters outside Richmond. Within 24 hours he was back in the Oval Office, with no one in Washington aware he had been away.

The rivers that flow into the Chesapeake are an important part the Bay's transportation network. And there are a lot of them! Starting in the extreme north, the Susquehanna flows from Pennsylvania into the narrow upper end. Down the Bay's Western Shore, eight rivers empty into its waters from Maryland: Gunpowder, Back, Patrapsco, Magothy, Severn, South, West, and Patuxent. Then there is the broad Potomac, which is the state line between Maryland and Virginia. In

Virginia, four more rivers flow into the Bay: Rappahannock, Pian-katank, York, and James. (The two most southerly rivers, first discov-ered by the early settlers, were named after English royalty, while the two further north were named later for local Indian tribes.)

On the Bay's Eastern Shore, eight more rivers feed the Bay. All are in Maryland. They are Bohemia, Sassafras, Chester, Eastern, Tred Avon, Choptank, Nanticoke, and Wicomico.

A visitor may be surprised to learn that Maryland has more than 3,100 miles of shoreline, but only 31 miles of it faces the Atlantic. This startling fact is explained by the many sounds and caves that form the Bay's jagged shoreline. There are literally hundreds of places on the Eastern Shore where two neighbors, facing each other's houses across a short expanse of water, can visit each other in minutes by boat, while the trip *around* the inlet could take an hour or more by car. (In Colonial times, that same journey would have taken a day or more by wagon.)

It will *not* surprise the visitor to the Chesapeake, therefore, to learn that in this topography where hundreds of fingers of water poke into the land from all directions, the *boat* still ranks high on the scale of must "things" to own, and a dock often exceeds a garage in importance. For the visitor, the boat is the "transport of delight" that will open up the wonders and pleasures of the Chesapeake.

As an inlet of the ocean, the Bay pulses with the ebb and flow of the ocean's tides, although the Atlantic, with such a mighty basin to fill and empty twice each day, achieves a tidal range of only 2 to 3 feet from high to low. For large ships, smaller commercial vessels operating between local ports, the "watermen" who earn their living on Bay waters, and for small-boat recreational sailors, this small tidal range is a blessing. While sailors to the north and south of the Chesapeake—from Maine to Georgia—contend with tides that rise and fall 6 to 8 feet, and must have floating docks to accommodate the change, Chesapeake sailors simply moore their boats with a careful arrangement of docking lines.

The Chesapeake is more than a boon to water transportation. Being *salt* water—because of the ebb and flow of the tide—the Bay is home to a marvelous variety of seafood—the fish, clams, crabs and oysters that have been taken out of the Bay for centuries. At the time of the earliest settlements, the water was so pure and the Bay so full of seafood that had reproduced for centuries undisturbed (with the exception of small amounts consumed by local Indians) that boatloads of seafood were the "miracle" that helped Jamestown survive until its first crops were harvested. The Bay has continued to provide such delicacies right up to the present, although warnings are beginning to appear.

Some years ago, when the internal combustion engine was developed and the sailboats of the Bay were first converted to power, it became evident that Chesapeake oysters, which were being shipped in ice all over the country, would not last long if powerboats were allowed to dredge them off the bottom. So a law was passed that oysters could only be dredged by boats under *sail power alone.* And so it remains today, to the delight of visitors, who occasionally see them working offshore or watch them returning to their home ports at night.

Industrial pollution is another threat to Bay waters, but it is gratifying to report that surrounding states and the federal government are making a concerted and costly effort to curtail contamination. Unless they succeed, one of the Chesapeake's greatest gifts, its seafood, will be lost to the Bay's residents and to millions of others along the Eastern Seaboard.

Geographically, the Chesapeake ebbs and flows through two states, the upper 60 percent of it in Maryland, the lower 40 percent in Virginia. The dividing line lies—like the border between North and South Korea —on the 38th Parallel of Latitude. On the Western Shore, the state line follows the Potomac River. Let's look at the land around the Chesapeake. Later chapters will follow this clockwise exploration of the Bay.

Maryland was founded as a English colony in 1634 by Cecil Calvert, the second Lord Baltimore. It was named for Queen Henrietta Maria. Calvert was a Roman Catholic who believed in religious freedom, and the new colony was open to all faiths. The settlements were ruled by succeeding Lords Baltimore through the Colonial period. During the American Revolution, the Second Continental Congress met briefly in Baltimore. The new federal government sat for a time in Annapolis, until the state gave land for the District of Columbia.

During the War of 1812, while watching ships of the Royal Navy shell Fort McHenry in Baltimore Harbor, Francis Scott Key wrote the words to the "Star Spangled Banner," and the song became our national anthem. By that time, Maryland was already known as the "Old Line State," a nickname given it when George Washington praised the heroic "troops of the line" for their fighting prowess during the Revolution. Half a century later, during America's Civil War, 60 percent of the battles were fought in Virginia, but several major engagements took place in Maryland, including one of the bloodiest: Antietam.

Maryland has a population of 4.2 million, with nearly 9 out of 10 citizens living in rural areas. The state has its highest point at Backbone Mt. (3,360 ft.), and its lowest, sea level, on its Atlantic shore. Maryland's motto is *Fatti Machii Parole Femine* ("Manly deeds, womanly words"), and the state song is "Maryland, My Maryland" (to the melody of the German "O, Tannenbaum"). Maryland's state bird, not surprisingly, is the Baltimore Oriole, its flower is the Black-Eyed Susan, and its tree is the White Oak.

On its farms, Maryland grows corn, soybeans, and tobacco, and produces milk, broilers, and beef cattle. In its factories, the output is electric and electronic equipment, machinery, chemicals, transportation equipment, printed materials, paper products, and clothing; and from its mines, clay, stone, coal, sand, and gravel.

Virginia, at the southern end of the Chesapeake, has nearly four times the land area of Maryland (39,700 to 10,577 square miles), with a high point in its western mountains at Mt. Rogers (5,729 ft.), and a low point, like Maryland, on the Atlantic Shore. The population of the "Old Dominion" is 5.3 million. Virginia was named for Elizabeth I, the "Virgin Queen" of England. As noted above, Jamestown (1607), on the James River, was the first permanent English settlement in America. When Virginia entered the Union on June 25, 1788, it covered an enormous land area that extended all the way to the Mississippi River. This area was eventually carved up into eight of our present states.

Small details of interest are: state flower—American dogwood; state bird—Cardinal; state dog—Foxhound; state motto—*Sic Semper Tyrannis* ("Thus always to tyrants"); and state song—"Carry Me Back to Old Virginia."

The Lure of the Chesapeake

When you arrive at the Bay, you'll find that the focus, carried over from the area's earliest days, is on *water,* all the things you can do in, on, and around the water. And that means boats. Not *only* boats, of course, because a great many attractions are *at* the water's edge—fishing piers, waterfront restaurants, port facilities, fishing stations, art galleries, craft fairs, and theaters. But if you want to enjoy the Chesapeake to the fullest, make sure you include boats in your plans.

In many Chesapeake port towns, a boat ride is simply the *best* way to get from here to there or to see the sights, perhaps the only way to get the full picture. Many towns and cities—Baltimore and Annapolis come to mind—recognize this and their harbor boat tours are among their most popular offerings. Most boat rides run an hour or less, but you *can* find longer boat tours. Some boat rides will take you out on the Bay for a whole day (with lunch or dinner aboard), and you can even cruise for a week, living aboard as you would on a mini ocean liner.

For visitors who arrive already in love with boats—perhaps owning one back home—the problem is not where to find them, but how to keep boating activities within your available time.

Let's say you've taken in Baltimore—done the Inner Harbor tour; gone aboard the U.S. Navy's first ship, the U.S.S. *Constellation;* toured the fabulous new Aquarium; explored the shops; and sampled the restaurant fare—and now you are ready to move on. Head south!

About 50 miles south on Rt. 2 lies Annapolis, the state capital, site of many historic buildings, home of the U.S. Naval Academy, and headquarters of more "boating activity" than you can wave an oar at. Here, in the summer season, you may see a sailing regatta, take a harbor ride, rent a boat for fishing, charter a sailboat for a day or a week of sailing on your own, check out dozens of yacht brokers (for a used boat) or boat dealers (for a new one), or thump hulls the way car buffs love to kick tires at auto shows. If you're a boat person, wander from showroom to boatyard and back to showroom to see which one of them is offering your next "dreamboat." If you're already a boat-owner, the next step in your cruising life is a custom-built boat and you can easily spend an entire Chesapeake vacation discussing your requirements (and the cost) with boatbuilders in and around the Annapolis area. They're tucked into every nook and cranny around the Severn and South Rivers, which flow into the Bay on either side of town.

In spite of this small port-town's Colonial heritage, it's no exaggeration to say that Annapolis is the most boat- and boating-oriented town on the U.S. East Coast. (Although Newport, Rhode Island, might take exception.) If you're there in mid-October, when *two* four-day boat shows are held (Sail, then Power), back to back, you'll understand why Chesapeake Bay sailors are called "serious boating people." Wherever there isn't a boat dealer or charter operation or boatyard, you'll find a sail loft or a ship's chandlery offering all sorts of salty and sophisticated yacht gear. If you are planning to attend the Annapolis boat shows, make sure you make your lodging reservation *not less than six months in advance;* Annapolis is awash with yachting types during the middle two weekends in October!

Across the Bay (via the bridge), two real boating towns recommend themselves to the boat-lover. Set in the more placid country of the Eastern Shore and home ports to many beautifully maintained wood boats of classical vintage, these towns are Cambridge and Oxford, both dating back to Colonial days, as their English names suggest. After crossing the Bay Bridge, you drive south on US 50, turning off on Rt. 333 to reach Oxford; then, returning to US 50, drive south again, across the Choptank River into Cambridge. Both towns are renowned for gracious inns offering comfortable "Old World" accommodations and menus filled with Chesapeake gourmet delicacies.

The remainder of the Eastern Shore, down through the rest of Maryland and Virginia to Cape Charles and the Bay Bridge and Tunnel complex, is a quiet agricultural region, with many small farms, some large estates, and few towns of any real size. The shoreline through here is cut by rivers that flow through marshland to the Bay. Each peninsula formed by two rivers is as jagged as an octopus—miles and miles of twisting shoreline, creating dozens of small bays and sounds. It's a watery playground made in heaven for the small-boat sailor, the professional "waterman" who makes his living from the Bay's offerings, and for the amateur who cruises for pleasure or fishes for sport. Dozens of country roads end at the water's edge, where you may find a small boatyard, a town dock, a public launching ramp, a small boat club—or just a few boats tied up to stakes, waiting there until their owners are free to go fishing or sailing again. In almost every town, however small, you'll find some type of "eatery," from a simple lunch stand on the water's edge to a pleasant Bay-front restaurant. Count on it—each will be serving fresh-caught seafood from the Bay.

If you cross the Delmarva Peninsula toward the ocean (from Cambridge, take US 50 to Salisbury and stay on it till you reach the ocean), you can visit Ocean City, Maryland's only seaside resort. Ocean City is for swimming in ocean surf (10 miles of beach) or strolling along the Boardwalk. Then, turning south again toward Cape Charles, you can stop at Chincoteague, Virginia, to savor Tom's Cove oysters, touted by the natives as "the best in the world." And here at Chincoteague, in the fall of the year, you may be on hand when the wild ponies that live on Assateague Island are herded for a swim to the mainland, where they are auctioned off to the highest bidders. You can go ocean fishing here on a "head boat" (up to 30 people) or a "charter boat" (up to 6), and you can do the same further down the coast in Wachapreague, as you head for the Bay Bridge-Tunnel.

For those who like a taste of small-town flavor, pause a while at Oyster (pronounced "Orster" locally)—perhaps for lunch—to take in the daily routine of folks who face the ocean with their backs to the Bay, and make a living from both. In Oyster you'll find piles of oyster shells that are higher than your head down by the waterfront, evidence from decades of making a living from the town's namesake. And here there's a wonderful seafood festival every year in the autumn.

After that, your next jump south will take you over *and* under the Bay on the toll bridge-tunnel into Norfolk. There, in the harbor you can take a boat trip and see the U.S. Navy's mothballed fleet and vessels of every description crisscrossing the Bay and harbor. In nearby Virginia Beach, Hampton, and Newport News, you'll find a wide range of cultural activities, historic sites, and, yes, more seafood restaurants. As you cross another (toll) bridge-tunnel to Hampton and drive northward, you should be aware that just a few miles inland to the west, Virginia offers a great concentration of historical sites (more on these below).

If you turn northward on US 17, veering eastward back toward the Bay, and across the Piankatank River, you'll arrive in Deltaville, a town widely known as the capital of wooden boatbuilding on Virginia's Western Shore. For those who like to study local types and see steel and wood boats under construction, more than half a dozen boatyards are turning out yachts and the boats that local watermen use for their work on the Bay. There's more of the same if you follow the Rappahannock River upstream to Urbanna, but if you don't want to wander too far inland, you can cross the Piankatank on the Rt. 3 bridge into Lancaster and Northumberland Counties. This region, like that south of it, is tobacco country, and here you will find Reedville and Smith Point, where you can catch ferries bound across the Bay with stops at islands in mid-Bay. Interstate 64, north out of Norfolk, will take you to that historic trio—Jamestown, Williamsburg, and Yorktown.

Further north in Virginia's Northern Neck, the next river crossing is over the wide Potomac, where there are no bridges until you reach US 301. For those who wish to take in some American history, a "detour" up Virginia Rt. 202 will bring you close to Stratford Hall, the birthplace of Robert E. Lee. (See more later on historic sites.) Either way, when you reach US 301, you can turn north again, cross the Potomac (toll bridge), and reenter Maryland. At this point you'll be about 50 miles south of Annapolis, the end of this imaginary circuit of the Bay. If you use this plan and arrive back at Annapolis with time left to spend, you can easily fill the remaining days taking in bypassed events and attractions in Maryland's capital.

FACTS
AT YOUR
FINGERTIPS

FACTS AT YOUR FINGERTIPS

 BOATS AND BOATING. When considering the Chesapeake, visitors should put boats and boating at (or near) the top of their list of attractions and things to do. To the recreational sailor, the Bay is a cruising ground par excellence with its hundreds of sheltered anchorages tucked in behind all those points of land—quiet places to relax at the end of the cruising day. To the boat *lover,* the Bay is dotted with hundreds of boatbuilders, charter boat operators, fishing boat rental stations, yacht brokers, new-boat dealers, yacht clubs, commercial vessels, and boatyards where a visitor can browse just for the pleasure of looking at boats. Boats of all kinds, for many purposes, is what the Bay and its people are all about. Yet boats are only part of the Chesapeake picture. To the lover of good food, especially regional seafood specialties and time-proven Colonial dishes, the Chesapeake is dotted along both shores with charming rural inns, urban restaurants, and waterfront "eateries" that offer gourmet seafood dishes made from the day's catches in the Bay—fish, crab, clams, and oysters.

Boat- and water-lovers' intent on absorbing the Bay's nautical ambiance but also interested in the hallowed sites of great events in history, need only journey inland a few miles from the water to discover much of America's past. When Captain John Smith explored the Bay from Jamestown in 1608 he was so delighted by what he found—protected coves, abundant seafood, tree-covered islands, and gentle woods and fields—that he named one of the islands after himself. (It lies between Smith Point, VA, and Crisfield, MD, and visitors can reach it by ferry.) Allowing for some changes over nearly four centuries, today's visitor will find Chesapeake Bay no less entrancing.

 WHEN TO GO. The Chesapeake lies in the mid-Atlantic region, definitely offering a "Southern" climate during the summer months, with appreciable humidity, yet having a rather mild spring and fall. "A good time to visit" spans nine to ten months of the year. Water has a strongly moderating influence on temperature; it's often warmer inland, but it's more humid near the water. A spring or fall vacation has its advantages if you don't mind slipping into a sweater or windbreaker when it becomes cool in the late afternoon—there is a welcome decrease in the size of crowds at most attractions and historical sites during the off-season months. Also, there are often price decreases during the "off" season.

The other side of the weather coin is that you *will,* as noted, encounter sticky heat during the summer. Washington, near the Chesapeake, and Baltimore on the Bay are famous—or infamous—for their humidity, and that condition applies to the whole Chesapeake area. The saving grace, at least some of the time, is that when you're on or near the water a cooling breeze often takes some of the sting out of the heat.

As for Places to See and Things to Do, there's a jam-packed Calendar of Events in both states from one end of the year to the other. A visitor won't find winter an inappropriate time for a Chesapeake vacation.

Weather in the Bay area is relatively mild throughout the year. Winters average 45°F; summers are in the 80°F range, but the humidity often makes it feel much warmer.

 PLANNING YOUR TRIP. If you're coming from the Northeast or from Southern states, and have the time to skirt the entire Bay on your vacation, the logical starting points are Havre de Grace or Baltimore in the north, and Norfolk in the south. If you're driving and choose one of these, a complete circuit of the Bay will land you at your starting point for the trip home. From the northwest (Pennsylvania) or west (West Virginia), the logical starting points are Baltimore or Washington, D.C. If available vacation time makes a circuit of the Bay too ambitious, you can tour *half* the Bay area, say the upper half for northern visitors and the lower half for Southerners, thus saving driving time that can be used visiting sites. But keep in mind that the *two* Bay crossings are almost 150 miles apart (the Bay bridge at Annapolis and the Bridge-Tunnel at Norfolk), so if you drive very far north from Norfolk, or south from Baltimore or Annapolis, you will have a fairly long haul by road before you reach the next crossing. On the Bay's Western Shore, the Potomac River is the dividing line between the two states, and it's so broad at its mouth that there are no bridges until you've driven 45 miles upriver.

Don't count on a "shorefront" drive where you will always have the Bay in sight. There are only a few places where this is possible. The best way to see the Bay by car is to visit the waterfront towns that attract you and stop at or near them for lodgings and meals.

As for accessibility, the Bay area is well served from all directions by Interstate highways and excellent U.S. and state roads: from the north, by I-81, I-83, and state roads; from the northeast, the same two interstates and I-95; from the west, I-64, I-70, and US 50 are the best choices, and from the south, the lower end of I-95 is the natural route. It skirts the Bay's Western Shore from top to bottom, while US 13 and 50 bisect the Eastern Shore, north to south (and vice versa, of course).

Northern visitors who approach the Eastern Shore of the Bay (after crossing the Delaware Memorial Bridge from New Jersey into Maryland), follow US 301 to reach US 50, which curves down the Delmarva Peninsula, inland but parallel to the Bay as far as Salisbury, Maryland, where it meets US 13. US 13 soon dips south into Virginia for an easy drive to the Bay Bridge and Tunnel, which crosses the mouth of the Chesapeake to Norfolk.

New Jersey motorists may find it interesting, even quicker, to take the toll ferry from Cape May to Cape Henlopen, DE, rather than crossing the Delaware further north at the Memorial Bridge. And from the South, those bound for the Bay's Eastern Shore can choose any highway leading to Norfolk; especially Rts.

17, 13, and 58. Rts. 17 and 13 cross at Norfolk, with Rt. 17 tending northwest up Virginia's North Neck until it meets US 301 near Port Royal.

By Bus. There are four major cities on or near the Bay where one might logically start a tour: Baltimore, Washington, Annapolis, and Norfolk. But it must be said that after you have arrived at one of these cities, by Greyhound or Trailways, any real appreciation of the Bay's attractions pretty much requires a car. The sole exception might be a split-week spent in Baltimore and Annapolis, arriving in one, and a few days later taking a bus to finish the week in the other.

By Train. Reliable and frequent AMTRAK service is available to the cities listed above (except Annapolis), but the visitor still faces the same problem mentioned above: reaching the Bay's waterfront restaurants, colonial sites, and historic landmarks demands a car.

By Air. The best arrival points, those served by most major airlines, are the Baltimore-Washington International Airport, lying midway between those two cities, National Airport in Washington, and Norfolk. The obvious choice for foreign visitors arriving on an international flight is Baltimore-Washington International. From there it would be convenient to include a few days in the nation's capital before beginning a Chesapeake Bay tour at Baltimore's restored Inner Harbor, with its shops, ships, and seafood, or a bit further south at historic Annapolis.

TOURIST INFORMATION. For additional information to plan your Chesapeake trip, the following addresses will be helpful. They are listed with Maryland first, by Western Shore counties that face the Bay, then Eastern Shore; after that, the useful Virginia addresses. NOTE: When writing for tourist information about the Virginia section of the Delmarva Peninsula, specify that you're interested in *Virginia's* Eastern Shore.

MARYLAND

Western Shore. *Baltimore City*—Baltimore Office of Promotion & Tourism, 110 W. Baltimore St., Baltimore, MD 21201; (301) 752–8632 or 837–INFO (24-hr. information). *Harford County*—Discover Harford County, P.O. Box 635, Bel Air, MD 21014; (301) 836–8986. *Baltimore County*—Chamber of Commerce, 100 W. Pennsylvania Ave., Towson, MD 21204; (301) 825–6200. *Annapolis & Anne Arundel County*—Tourism Council, P.O. Box 190, Owings, MD 20736; (301) 535–1013. *St. Mary's County*—Dept. of Tourism, P.O. Box 351, Leonardtown, MD 20650; (301) 475–5621.

Eastern Shore (MD). *Cecil County*—Office of Planning, County Office Bldg., Rm. 300, Elkton, MD 21621; (301) 398–0200, Ext. 144. *Kent, Queen Anne's & Talbot Counties*—Tourism Council of the Upper Chesapeake, P.O. Box 66, Centreville, MD 21617; (301) 758–2300. *Dorchester County*—Dorchester County Tourism, P.O. Box 307, Cambridge, MD 21613; (301) 228–3234. *Wicomico County*—Convention & Visitor's Bureau, Glen Ave. Ext., Salisbury, MD 21801;

(301) 546–3466 or 749–TOUR (24-hr. information). *Somerset County*—Tourism Commission, P.O. Box 243, Princess Anne, MD 21853; (301) 651–2968.

VIRGINIA

Virginia's comprehensive tourism program offers nearly 600 pamphlets to visitors on all areas and activities of the state. Many fascinating Colonial, Revolutionary War, and Civil War sites lie in Virginia and a fair number of these are close to the Bay. Here are some useful addresses for information on your Virginia trip: Virginia Travel Council, P.O. Box 15067, Richmond, VA 23227; (804) 786–0444, or Virginia Div. of Tourism, 202 N. Ninth St., Suite 500, Richmond, VA 23219; (804) 786–4484.

When writing or calling for assistance, be sure to describe your primary interests, so either states' tourism offices can send you the most approriate material.

 HINTS FOR MOTORISTS. Both Maryland and Virginia, of course, have the 55 mph speed limit, and Maryland has a reputation for being tough on speeders: a word to the wise should be sufficient! Remember, you're on vacation, out to have fun, see interesting sights, and *relax*. There's no need for a heavy foot on the gas pedal.

HIGHWAY INFORMATION CENTERS

On the Road in Maryland. Once you have arrived in Maryland, there are four highway information centers available to make your trip a success: 1. On I-95, near Laurel (up north), in the Rest Area at Mile Marker 37, serving southbound and northbound traffic; it's open Memorial Day to Labor Day, 8:30–6:30, but is closed Thanksgiving, Christmas, New Year's Day, and Easter. 2. On I-95 in Cecil County, in the Rest Area at Mile Marker 29, serving traffic headed both ways; open weekdays 9–5; weekends and holidays 8–4; closed same holidays as above. 3. State House Visitors' Center, in Maryland State House, State Circle, Annapolis; open daily 9–5; closed same holidays as above. 4. US 13 Information Center, located on Route 13 (Eastern Shore), 2 mi. north of the Virginia state line on the Delmarva Peninsula.

On the Road in Virginia. There are 10 locations in Virginia where the motorist can get help in planning a Chesapeake tour, and where the wide selection of brochures mentioned above are available. They are located as follows: *Northern Region*—On I-81 in Clear Brook, and on I-66 in Manassas; *Northeastern Region*—on I-95 in Fredricksburg; *Tidewater Region*—On US 13 in New Church (Delmarva); *South-Central Region*—On I-95 in Skippers, and on I-85 in Bracey; *Southwest Region*—On I-81 in Bristol, and on I-77 in Lambsburg; *Western Region*—On I-64 in Covington. In general terms, this means there is a Welcome Center on every interstate highway just inside the Virginia state line.

TIPS FOR BRITISH VISITORS. Passports. You will need a valid passport and a U.S. visa (which can only be put in a passport of the 10-year-kind). The type and validity of U.S. visas vary considerably; detailed information should be obtained from the nearest U.S. Embassy or Consulate. You can obtain the visa either through your travel agent, or directly from the *United States Embassy,* Visa and Immigration Department, 5 Upper Grosvenor St., London W1 (tel. 01–499 5521).

No vaccinations are required for entry into the U.S.

Customs. If you are 21 or over, you can take into the U.S.: 200 cigarettes or 50 cigars or 3 lbs. of tobacco (combination of proportionte parts permitted); and 1 U.S. quart of alcohol. In addition, every visitor, including minors, is allowed duty-free gifts to a value of $100. No alcohol or cigarettes may be included in this gift exemption, but up to 100 cigars may be. Be careful not to take in meat or meat products, seeds, plants, fruits, etc. Avoid narcotics like the plague.

Insurance. We heartily recommend that you insure yourself to cover health and motoring mishaps, with *Europ Assistance,* 252 High St., Croydon CRO 1NF (tel. 01–680 1234). Their excellent service is all the more valuable when you consider the possible costs of health care in the U.S.

Air Fares. We suggest you explore the current scene for budget flight possibilities—APEX and other fares offer considerable saving over the full price. Quite frankly, only business travelers who don't have to watch the price of their tickets fly full price these days—and find themselves sitting right beside APEX passengers!

TIPS FOR DISABLED TRAVELERS. Both Maryland and Virginia, which play host to hordes of visitors every year, have made significant strides in adapting their attractions to the needs of the disabled. The Maryland Travel Guide (Office of Tourist Development, 45 Calvert St., Annapolis, MD 21401, (301) 269–3517), for instance, lists 16 types of handicapped facilities that have been incorporated into public and private attractions. These include such conveniences as barrier-free access, ramps, handrails, reserved parking spaces, and accessible phones, elevators, bathrooms, drinking fountains, assembly areas, and turnstiles. Naturally all these are not offered at *every* site, but the program continues along with the awareness of its importance, especially in new construction.

In Virginia, special efforts have been made to accommodate the disabled visitor. The number of state attractions that have been made accessible—121 in all—includes such sites and attractions as air shows, national battlefields, vineyards, state and national parks, churches, plantations, botanical gardens, Indian reservations, wildlife refuges, museums, zoological parks, theaters, boat cruises, and seashore areas. A helpful brochure for planning a trip is "Tips For The Disabled Traveler," available from: Div. of Tourism, 202 N. Ninth St., Suite 500, Richmond, VA 23219; (804) 786–2051.

TIME ZONE AND AREA CODES. Both states are in the Eastern Standard Time Zone, and go on and off Daylight Saving Time in April and October. Maryland has only one telephone area code (301) for the entire state, but Virginia has two, (703) in the western and northern part, and (804) in the south and along the Eastern Shore, i.e., the Chesapeake area.

RECOMMENDED READING. For those who like to do a little "homework" before a trip, here are a few useful books to broaden your knowledge of the two states:

Maryland. *Maryland: A Bicentennial History,* by Carl Bode, published by W. W. Norton, New York, 1978.

Maryland Folklore and Folklife, by George C. Carey, published by Cornell Maritime Press, 1970.

Portrait of a Free State, by Donald M. Dozen, published by Cornell Maritime Press, 1976.

For a fictionalized but fine rendering of the Bay's special flavor, don't forget James Michener's best-seller, *Chesapeake.*

And for lovers of crab, *The Official Crab Eater's Guide,* by Whitey Schmidt, Marian Hartnett Press, Alexandria, VA, 1985.

Virginia. *Virginia, A Guide to the Old Dominion,* by Hans Hannau, Oxford Univ. Press, New York, 1940.

Virginia, by Hans Hannau, Doubleday, Garden City, NY, 1966.

Virginia Beautiful, by Wallace Nutting, EPM Publications, McLean, VA, 1974.

When you reach the Chesapeake area, wherever you arrive, go to the local newsstand (perhaps in your motel/hotel lobby) and buy the current copy of **Chesapeake Bay Magazine.** At $2 an issue, it is an excellent guide and offers interesting articles on all aspects of Bay life. The magazine also lists restaurants and current events and provides a sweeping survey of everything the Bay area has to offer.

WHAT IT WILL COST. Generally, two people can travel in the USA for an average of $80 a day (not including gasoline and other transportation expenses), as you can see in the table below. Regionally, however, there are wide variations. The U.S. Northeast is the most expensive area, followed by the mid-Atlantic states, which includes the Chesapeake Bay area, followed by other sections of the country.

In many areas you can cut expenses by traveling off season, when hotel and motel rates are usually lower. The budget-minded traveler can often find bargain accommodations at family-style "Y's," but that's limited, of course, to larger cities. In the Chesapeake Bay region, especially in less-populated areas such as the Eastern Shore, there are tourist homes—even rooms for rent in private houses—that cost considerably less than commercial establishments. And over 250 colleges in 41 states offer dormitory rooming to tourists at single-room rates of $3 to $12 per night, with meals from $2 to $6. A directory of more than 200 such bargains across the U.S. is *Mort's Guide to Low-Cost Vacations & Lodgings on College Campuses, USA–Canada,* available from Mort Barrish Assoc., Research Park, State Rd., Princeton, NJ 08540.

Another way to cut the cost of your trip is to look for out-of-the-way resorts. Travelers are frequently rewarded by discovering attractive areas that have not yet begun to draw large crowds, thus offering accommodations at lower than prevailing rates.

Typical Expenses for Two People

Room at an *inexpensive* hotel or motel	$35
Breakfast, including tip	$ 5
Lunch at *inexpensive* restaurant, including tip	$ 8
Dinner at *moderate* restaurant, including tip	$20
Sightseeing harbor tour	$ 6
An evening drink	$ 4
Admission to museum or historic site	$ 2
	$80

If you are budgeting your trip, don't forget to set aside a realistic amount for the possible rental of recreational equipment such as fishing gear or a boat. Prices on the Chesapeake may vary widely, depending on location, but figure $8 to $12 for a full day. (If you own an outboard motor and take it along in your car's trunk, you can probably cut that figure in half. But remember, most fishing station operators will not let you mount more than a 15hp on their rental boats, so don't lug a 25hp model.) Also, allow for bridge, tunnel, and highway tolls, which can add up to a major expense. And don't forget extra film, suntan lotion, postcards and stamps, and other sundries—not to mention souvenirs.

After lodging, your biggest expense will be food, and here you can achieve impressive economies if you're willing to eat simply in your room or to picnic on the road. This will save both time and money, and may let you enjoy roadside stops that you might otherwise pass by. Before you leave home, assemble a picnic kit. Sturdy plastic plates, cups, and utensils are cheaper in the long run than throw-away paper. Pack a small electric coffee pot (or immersion heater) to use in your room at the start of the day, and two thermos bottles (one for hot, one for cold drinks). If you're traveling by car, it's wise to take along a small cooler. Even a larger camping icebox may fit into the trunk. Many roadside places sell ice by the cube or block. Convenient foods to carry include bread, milk, cold cereal, tea, instant coffee, bouillon cubes, instant soup packets, jam, peanut butter, fruit, fresh vegetables that need no cooking (lettuce, tomatoes, cucumbers, mushrooms, carrots), cold cuts, cheese, nuts, raisins, and eggs (hard-boiled in your room the night before). With just these you can eat conveniently and well and at a considerable saving for one or even two meals a day.

Even in restaurants there are cost-cutting tricks: 1) Always check the menu on the outside window or at the cash register for prices *before* you are seated.

2) Order a few standard items such as coffee, soup, or side dishes to test the price range and food quality. 3) Look around to see the size of portions and attractiveness of the servings other diners are receiving. 4) If it's not too much food for your appetite, order a *complete* dinner; à la carte *always* costs more. 5) If there's a salad bar or *smorgasbord,* fill up there and skip costly desserts. 6) Find a Chinese restaurant and order one less main dish than there are people in your group—and share; there's usually more than enough. 7) Ask about the "Daily" or "Chef's Special"; chances are it will be really good and a generous portion. 8) Don't forget that in many restaurants "lunch" may be a better bargain than dinner and *some* places will serve any dish all day (including breakfast dishes at noon). 9) Tell the waiter or waitress how much ice you want in a beverage; if you don't want much, you'll get at least 30 percent more to drink. 10) Don't hesitate to ask for a "refill" before you've finished your tea or coffee; there's rarely an extra charge.

If you like a drink before dinner or bed, bring your own bottle. Most hotels and motels provide free ice from ice makers in the hall, but the mark-up on alcoholic beverages in restaurants, bars, cocktail lounges, and dining rooms can be staggering. If you forget to bring your favorite libation from home, you can buy it in Virginia at one of the state-run ABC (Alcoholic Beverage Commission) stores. In Maryland, liquor is generally available.

SENIOR CITIZEN DISCOUNTS. Senior citizens may in some cases receive special discounts on lodgings. The Days Inn chain offers various discounts to those 55 and older. Holiday Inns extend a discount to NRTA members (write to National Retired Teachers Assn, Membership Div., 215 Long Beach Blvd., Long Beach, CA 90802, if you qualify) and to the AARP (American Assn. of Retired Persons, Membership Div., 215 Long Beach Blvd., Long Beach, CA 90802). The amounts and availability of discounts change, so it's wise to check in advance with these organizations or with the hotel or motel chain. The National Council of Senior Citizens, 925 15th St., N.W., Washington, D.C. 20005, is always working to develop low-cost travel opportunities for it members.

PLACES TO STAY. Accommodations around the Chesapeake vary widely and wildly in price. In major cities and popular tourist centers such as Baltimore, Williamsburg, Annapolis, and Norfolk, you can expect hotel and motel rooms to compare closely with similar city accommodations in the rest of the mid-Atlantic region. The same holds true for fashionable or long-established inns. This rule-of-thumb applies on both sides of the Bay. In less-densely populated areas (where taxes and real estate values are lower), also on both sides of the Bay near quiet ports and smaller towns, you'll often find lower nightly rates. (See below for a general scale of rates.) In Virginia, the Econo-Travel Motor Hotel chain—now numbering more than 40—is striving to bring low-priced rooming to the state.

It is difficult not to generalize about room rates; the variations are wide and somethimes capricious. Still, *in general,* we have tried in this guide to keep the visitor in mind, evaluating locations, facilities, and service against the money the traveler is expected to pay. Our moods and our pocketbooks often influence our judgments of the places we stay. The same is true of our enjoyment of the places we dine. As any lodging host or restauranteur knows: You'll never satisfy all of the people all of the time. Most of them try—and so have we.

So, our *very general* pricing structure throughout this guide is as follows, based on double occupancy: *Deluxe,* $100 or more; *Expensive,* $75–$100; *Moderate,* $40–$75; and *Inexpensive,* $40 or less.

Most major hotels accept most major credit cards; others accept but a few, or none. Many of our listings include those cards that we have learned are acceptable at a particular hotel, motel, or restaurant. These are indicated by the following abbreviations at the end of each selection:

AE - American Express
CB - Carte Blanche
DC - Diners Club
MC - MasterCard
V - Visa.

If none is listed, ask *before* you commit yourself. The omission may be ours, but it's also possible that the place at which you hope to eat or stay has a firm house policy: Greenbacks only!

Hotel and Motel Categories

Hotel and motel selections in the Fodor's guidebooks to cities, states, and regions in the United States are, as far as possible, arranged by price, usually for double occupancy. Keep in mind that the selection of accommodations in and around the Chesapeake Bay Vacationland is just that—a *selection* of hotels, motels, and inns in a variety of price categories. Keep in mind also that rates may change seasonally (or at the discretion of management), and a facility we list in one price range may slip into another while we're on press or before you read and use this guide.

Although the various hotel and motel categories are fairly standard throughout Fodor's U.S. guidebook series, the prices listed under each category may vary from one area to another. Such variations reflect local price standards; a *moderate* price in a large urban area might be considered quite *expensive* in a rural region. Our listings therefore are meant to guide and should not be taken as an absolute. Prices, where given, are the most recent reported to Fodor's editors by our representatives in the field.

Super Deluxe. This category is reserved for only a few resorts or exceptional hotels. In addition to offering the visitor all the amenities discussed under the deluxe category (below), the super deluxe hotel has a unique atmosphere of glamor, good taste, and superb service. In short, super deluxe is "the tops."

Deluxe. The minimum facilities here will include bath *and* shower in all rooms, valet and laundry service, suites available, a well-appointed restaurant and lounge (where local law permits), TV and telephone in room, air-conditioning and heat, pleasing decor, and an atmosphere of luxury, even elegance. There should be ample and personalized service. In a deluxe *motel,* there may be less service rendered by employees and more by machine (such as refrigerators or ice-making machines in your room), but there should be a minimum of do-it-yourself in a truly deluxe establishment.

Expensive. All rooms must have bath *or* shower. There should be a restaurant or coffee shop, TV available, telephone in room, heat and air-conditioning, and a pleasing decor. Although the decor may match that in a deluxe establishment, hotels and motels in this category often are designed for commercial travelers or for families in a hurry, and service may be somewhat impersonal. Valet and laundry service may not be available. Units in this category will be notable primarily for their convenient locations and functional character.

Moderate. Each room should have an attached bath or shower. There should be a restaurant or coffee shop, TV available, telephone in room, heat and air-conditioning, relatively convenient location, with clean and comfortable rooms and public areas. *Motels* in this category may not have attached bath or shower, may not have a restaurant or coffee shop (although one is usually nearby), and may have no public rooms.

Inexpensive. Nearby bath or shower, telephone available, and clean rooms are the minimum.

Free parking is assumed at all motels and motor hotels; you must pay for parking at most city hotels, except for a few that offer free parking to guests in premium rooms. *Baby-sitter* lists are always available in good hotels and motels, and *cribs* for children are always on hand—sometimes without charge, but more often at $1 or $2 a night. The charge for a *cot* in your room (to increase sleeping capacity) should be about $3 per night, but an *extra single bed* will add about $7 to your bill at better hotels and motels.

 PLACES TO EAT. The Chesapeake area is highly regarded for its regional seafood specialties in both Maryland and Virginia. Crabs caught in the Bay are justly famous (in the form of crab cakes, especially) and it's said around the Bay that any Chesapeake chef worthy of the name knows at least 20 ways to prepare crab. The upper end of the Bay, Maryland's part, is famous for its oysters—although sad to relate the supply may be thinning dangerously— and these are enjoyed on the half shell, in stews, fried and—mixed with spices and baked—as appetizers. Both ends of the Bay are renowned for fish dishes— broiled or fried—and this includes black drum, channel bass, flounder, bluefish, weakfish, plus a whole range of others that come from the ocean.

Down in Virginia waters, you'll enjoy almost the same menus as you'll find further north, with minor variations from one place to another. Besides seafood, Virginia is also famous for its ham, especially the smoked Smithfield variety, which has a reputation more than two centuries old. (Of course, Southern Maryland is justifiably proud of *its* local ham.) Many surviving dishes from Colonial cooks are still served. Don't be afraid to try them; you'll probably be delighted. Speaking of Bay crab (as we did above), *Crab Norfolk,* seasoned with salt, red and black pepper, and vinegar, then baked *en casserole,* is a favorite at the lower end of the Bay. At Smithfield, where those wonderful hams come from, they claim the flavor comes from allowing the hogs to roam free in the fields until autumn, when they are let into the peanut fields to fatten. It's the peanuts and the special curing method that give them their distinctive flavor. Virginia is also renowned for spoonbread, fried chicken, and beef from Black Angus cattle.

Over on the Bay's Eastern Shore, in both states, you'll find the menus leaning strongly toward seafood. Delmarva natives are incredulous at anyone who doesn't love fish, oysters, and crab. In this area there's also a regional dish called *White Potato Pie.* It's made with pototoes and tomatoes, skillfully blended with milk, butter, eggs, sugar, lemon, cinnamon, and nutmeg. Try it; it's a delight.

For those not excited by seafood, be assured that restaurant menus will always include plenty of entrees that you might find anywhere else in the country. The waitress or waiter may look at you strangely, but the cook will do his best.

Reservations. For evening dining, the best advice is to make reservations whenever possible. Some popular restaurants won't accept reservations. Most hotels and rural vacation places have set dining hours. For motel-stayers, life is simpler if the motel has a restaurant. If it hasn't, try to stay at one that has a restaurant nearby, preferably one that serves breakfast, lunch, and dinner.

Dress. Some restaurants are fussy about a customer's dress, particularly in the evening. For women, pants and pants suits are now almost universally acceptable. For men, the tie and jacket remain the standard, but turtleneck sweaters are becoming more common. Shorts are almost always frowned on for both men and women at the better dinner places. Standards of dress are becoming progressively more relaxed, so a neatly dressed customer will usually experience no problem. If in doubt about accepted dress at a particular establishment, call ahead. Roadside stands, turnpike restaurants and cafeterias, and some beach restaurants have no fixed standards of dress. If you're traveling with children, find out if a restaurant has a children's menu and commensurate prices.

Tipping. When figuring the tip on your check, base it on the total charges for the meal, not on the grand total if that includes sales tax. Don't tip on tax. Figure the percentage as you would at home—neither mean nor wildly extravagant.

Restaurants in this guide that are located in large metropolitan areas are not always categorized by type of cuisine, although we try to point out that a particular place specializes in Country, Seafood, French, Chinese, or perhaps Armenian. Restaurants of a general menu are usually listed as "American-International." Restaurants in less populated areas are much the same, with the principal categories based on price: *expensive, moderate,* and *inexpensive.* As a general rule, restaurants in metropolitan areas are higher priced, but many that feature an ethnic cuisine are surprisingly inexpensive. Limitations of space make it impossible to include every establishment in our selection of restaurants so we attempted wherever possible to provide a variety of "safe" places within each price range.

Restaurant Categories

Although the restaurant categories are standard in this guide, the price range within each category may vary from area to area. This variation reflects local price standards, and (like the hotel/motel example) takes into account that a *moderate* price in a large urban area might be considered *expensive* in a rural region. In such instances, the dollar ranges for each category are stated before the listing of establishments.

Super Deluxe. This category indicates an outstanding restaurant, lavishly decorated, with a superb wine list, excellent service, immaculate kitchens, and a large well-trained staff.

Deluxe. Many fine restaurants around the country fall into this category. It will have earned a well-deserved reputation for excellence, perhaps serving a house specialty or two for which it is famous. It will provide attentive service in a pleasing or unique setting. A deluxe restaurant will have a good wine list (where the law permits), and will be considered one of the best in town by the inhabitants.

Expensive. In addition to the expected dishes, it will offer one or two house specialties, a wine list and cocktails (where law permits), air-conditioning (unless the locale makes it unnecessary), a general reputation for very good food and an adequate staff, a pleasant or elegant decor, and appropriately dressed clientele.

Moderate. Cocktails, wine, and/or beer where the law permits, air-conditioning (locale not precluding), a clean kitchen, adequate staff, better-than-average service, and a general reputation for good, wholesome food.

Inexpensive. Wholesome or hearty food in a "safe" place, with prices that won't put its customers into bankruptcy.

 SEASONAL EVENTS. The number of things to see and do all around the edge of the Chesapeake, in both Maryland and Virginia, for all 12 months of the year, is simply staggering. The following selection is a *summary* only of a year's events, and we have only included those that have been conducted for several years running. Each state publishes its own official *Calendar of Events* complete with dates and details. To get the most up-to-date information, contact: **Maryland**—Office of Tourist Development, 45 Calvert St., Annapolis, MD; (301) 269–3517. **Virginia**—Virginia Div. of Tourism, 202 N. Ninth St., Suite 500, Richmond, VA 23219; (804) 786–4484.

January. As might be expected, Maryland's January events are principally indoors, such as the New Year's Eve Ball at Havre de Grace, a sportfishing show at Annapolis, and a Lee-Jackson Confederate Memorial Service in Baltimore—all in the first third of the month. In Virginia, most January events by coincidence are inland, away from the Bay.

February. Maryland opens the month with the Anne Arundel County Agricultural Week in Annapolis (exhibits, demonstrations, products) held at the Annapolis Mall, while Baltimore has the Maryland Antique Show & Sale at the Historical Society Building, the Winter Market at the Convention Center, and the Hunt Valley Antiques Show. In Virginia, the Annual Mid-Atlantic Sports & Boat Show is held at Virginia Beach during the second week (admission charged), by now a well-attended event that draws exhibitors and spectators from a wide area.

March. Baltimore features its annual St. Patrick's Day Celebration at the city's War Memorial Plaza, while Havre de Grace has a Duck Decoy Festival. In Virginia, the Annual Mid-Atlantic Wildfowl Festival (fee) is held at the seaside city of Virginia Beach, while Norfolk about mid-month holds its Annual St. Patrick's Day Celebration at Norfolk Festevents.

April. This month, spring comes to most of the Chesapeake, and that's evident by the swing to outdoor activities. Early in April, Baltimore holds an Arbor Day Celebration at the War Memorial Plaza, and an Easter Celebration (same location). Down in Annapolis, the Children's Festival (at the Mall) is a weekend event, featuring "showcase entertainment" for the entire family. At mid-month, Baltimore hosts the Chesapeake Antique Automobile Show (outdoors), sponsored by the Auto Club of America at the Street Car Museum. The Annapolis Spring Festival (parade, entertainment, etc.) is held the third weekend, and further south in Virginia, Jamestown opens its summer-long celebration of the first English colony in America, featuring the *Godspeed*, a reproduction of one of the three sailing vessels that made the 1607 voyage to these shores. Norfolk holds an Annual Children's Easter Festival at Norfolk Festevents and at Chincoteague, over on the Delmarva Peninsula, there's a Decoy Carver Festival, at which local carvers competed for top honors. Norfolk fills April's third weekend with its highly regarded International Azalea Festival, held at the city's Council Building.

May. Maryland listed no less than 67 events in May last year and Virginia 46, so it's clear that spring has arrived on the Chesapeake. Virginia opens the month with the Annual Seafood Festival in Chincoteague, while Jamestown celebrates "Settlement Day" on with crafts, games, music, and military drills at the Jamestown Festival Park (fee). At Norfolk, the Ghent Arts Festival, held during an early weekend, features painting, sculpture, tapestries, leather goods, and photography at the Convention & Visitors' Bureau. Chincoteague *starts* the town's summer programs (running into early Sept.) at the Memorial Wildlife Refuge with nature walks, movies, lectures, and family activities. In Maryland, the May festivities often start with Baltimore's Flower Mart, a rite of spring dating back to 1911, offering visitors plants, flowers, arts, crafts, food, and entertainment at Mt. Vernon Place. Over in Ocean City (Delmarva), the Sweet Adelines Competition & Show fills a weekend with barbershop quartets and choruses. Baltimore holds its May Day celebration, a traditional folk event with a Maypole dance, at the Cloisters Children's Museum and there is a weekend Spring Festival at Havre de Grace's Steppingstone Museum, offering a horse and carriage show, exhibits of rural tools and crafts of the 1880–1920 period, and entertainment. Baltimore holds its Antiques Show at the city's Museum of Art, while in Annapolis, about midmonth, the U.S. Naval Academy's 6-day Commissioning Week includes parades, athletic events, and colorful ceremonies leading up to the graduation of the Academy's midshipmen. Also in May there is the annual Running of the Preakness Stakes (the middle event of thoroughbred racing's Triple Crown) at Pimlico Race Course. In the latter half of May, Baltimore holds a Bach Festival and Annapolis has its Roses & May Flowers Day.

June. This is another big month in Maryland and Virginia. Virginia starts with Harborfest at Norfolk, featuring tall ships, sailboat races, entertainment, children's activities, and seafood specialties. Portsmouth, Norfolk's neighbor across the harbor, holds its Annual Seawall Art Festival. About a week later, Colonial Beach (up the Potomac from the Bay) has its Annual Potomac River Festival. Virginia Beach stages its Boardwalk Art Show in June, featuring the works of artists and artisans along eight blocks of waterfront. In Maryland, Baltimore begins a summer-long series of international festivals called Showcase of Nations (through Sept.), staged its Dundalk Outdoor Art Show, and celebrates Confederate Memorial Day. At Hooper's Island (Eastern Shore), Fishing Tournament is sponsored by the VFW. Then Cambridge, also on the Eastern Shore, has its Strawberry Festival. At the lower end of Maryland's part of Delmarva, Pocomoke City has a Cypress Festival, while Crisfield—on the Bay —holds its Chamber of Commerce Fishing Tournament, offering thousands in prize money for the best catches in these categories: trout, flounder, croaker, bluefish and black drum.

July. On or around July 4, both states stage celebrations of Independence Day at so many locations you probably couldn't miss one wherever you are. Virtually all include parades, fireworks, contests, children's activities, and patriotic music. In Wachapreague, VA, they load the first two weeks with their Annual Art Show and Annual Eastern Shore Marlin Club Tournament. Nearby, in Chincoteague, the famous ponies of Assateague Island are herded (by local firemen) on their swim across the channel to the mainland, where an auction is held for all visitors who want to buy a pony. In Maryland, July's variety of attractions continues with a Canal Day Festival at the far northern end of the Bay in Chesapeake City, and at Baltimore with the Chesapeake Turtle Derby (10 classes racing for prizes and the crowning of a Grand Champ). In St. Mary's City (Western Shore, near the Potomac), the final two weeks of the month are given over to the Bay County Camp of the Theater Arts, and across the Bay, Easton holds the Talbot County Fair. A late July Eastern Shore special attraction in Cambridge is the Sail Regatta, followed by a Power Boat Regatta (races and a boat show).

August. On Virginia's Eastern Shore, Onancock holds a Harbor Festival (street dancing, Hobie Cat races, arts, crafts, and music), Virginia Beach stages its Folk Arts Festival, and Colonial Beach (on the Potomac) presents its Annual Boardwalk Art & Craft Show. Across the Bay on the Eastern Shore, Wachapreague has an Annual Fish Fry. August is a blockbuster month in Maryland. The Greater Baltimore Civil War Show & Sale is held in Towson (a suburb), featuring memorabilia from the War Between the States, while Havre de Grace holds hydroplane races on the Susquehanna and a Seafood Festival. Cambridge (Eastern Shore) also has a Seafood Festival, and the Dorchester (county) Fest on the Choptank River, an antique show with arts and crafts, Nanticoke Indians, bike races, tours, and water activities, is held at the Long Wharf and Armory. At Annapolis, there is the Kennel Club Dog Show & Trial and a 10K race through the historic district, both usually late in August. Edgewater (next to Annapolis) holds its Summer Evening Candlelight Tour of the National Historic Landmark, Ferry Tavern—18th Century music and refreshments—at the London Town Publik House. Crisfield in August hosts the National Hard Crab Derby (crab races, concerts, boat rides, and food) at the American Legion grounds, and the Miller High Life Mud Hop, with 10 classes of 4-wheel-drive vehicles competing for prizes over a muddy, rutted course.

September. In Maryland, Cambridge opens with its Aviation Day (sky diving, aerobatics, and model planes), Annapolis has a Seafood Festival, and Baltimore stages an "I Am An American" parade and Defenders' Day Celebration (the Anniversary of the Battle of Baltimore—War of 1812). Closing out the month, Havre de Grace has its Fall Harvest Festival, while at St. Clement's Island, up the Potomac from the Bay, there is a special event for boat lovers, the Blessing of the Fleet (oyster boats) with a ferry ride from Clements to the island, a historic pageant, entertainment, a horse-pull contest, and an abundance of local food. In Virginia, Cape Charles (Delmarva) holds Cape Charles Day (parades, marathon, and local arts and crafts, a flea market, and the "finest clam fritters around"), while Virginia Beach stages its Annual Neptune Festival (sand castle contests, parades, and entertainment). Portsmouth presents in September its National Hunting & Fishing Weekend (skeet-shooting, camping and ecology exhibits, and hunting dog demonstrations).

October. This month hardly feels like autumn in the Bay area, so it's no surprise that Virginia is still active with outdoor events through the month. Inland, off the Bay, it is fall foliage time, with harvest festivals (for apples, molasses, and tobacco), but in Chincoteague on the Eastern Shore, the big repeat event is an Oyster Festival ("oysters cooked every way"). Around Halloween, Portsmouth holds Olde Town Ghost Walk ("theatrical portrayals of ghosts, legends, and myths"), while Norfolk presents its Annual Halloween Celebration at Festevents, an adult costume ball with music, dancing, and food. In Maryland, Annapolis is the magnet for small-boat sailors as the Sailboat and Powerboat Shows take over the town for four days each at the Town Dock. At St. Michael's (Eastern Shore, below the Bay bridge), there is a Seafood Festival (besides the local catch, it includes crab races and entertainment), and at St. Mary's City (back on the Western Shore), there is the Old State House Quilt Show, held at the Reconstructed State House of 1676. Baltimore calls its autumn event Festival-On-The-Hill (in the city's premier Victorian neighborhoods), and Solomons, a popular Bay port, stages its Patuxent River Appreciation Days (nautical exhibits, boat rides, parade, and local foods). At Edgewater, the Needlework Show features a competition of outstanding needlework from the area, while down in St. Mary's City they celebrate Aboriginal

Life Day (an "exploration of prehistoric Indian lifeways"). Baltimore's Halloween Parade closes out the month.

November. In Maryland, Easton (just inland from St. Michaels on the Bay) holds a three-day Waterfowl Festival (featuring decoys and waterfowl art, guns, and a goose-calling contest), so you know that the millions of migratory birds that visit the Chesapeake each fall are expected soon. In Cambridge there is an Antique Show & Sale at the American Legion Post, and Baltimore holds its Mayor's Thanksgiving Celebration. In Virginia, Urbanna (up the Rappahannock from the Bay), holds an Oyster Festival with a parade, a 10K race, arts & crafts, and "special foods." Over on the Eastern Shore again, Chincoteague celebrates Waterfowl Week (right up to Dec. 1), at which nature trails at the Wildlife Refuge are open "as Canada and Snow Geese migrate south."

December. This is the month of Christmas, and both states load their calendars with Yuletide celebrations. Christmas festivities vary from carol and choral singing, tree lightings, candlelight tours, hot cider, and wassail cups to madrigal singers, courtly dancing, and recreated 18th Century customs. Norfolk also holds its Annual Waterfront New Year's Eve Festival (music, dancing, and fireworks) at Festevents. And in Maryland, Baltimore's Marathon is held early in the month at Memorial Stadium (thus demonstrating again the mildness of this season). Annapolis holds a mid-December Candlelight Pub Crawl, with guides in colonial costume leading the crowd on a tour of historic taverns, and Baltimore closes out the year's events with a New Year's Eve Extravaganza, with dozens of celebrations throughout the city, culminating in a fireworks display at the Inner Harbor.

It may be a cliché, but it's nevertheless true that the Chesapeake has something of interest or entertainment going on for every visitor all year long. And remember, the listings above are only a *sampling* of what the two new calendars will include.

RECREATIONAL ACTIVITIES

The focus here for a Chesapeake Bay visitor is on activities centered in, on, and around the water. This emphasis is continued in the final part of this opening section, *Historical Sites* (below), which includes Colonial *and* nautical points of interest in both states.

 SWIMMING. The impulse to go swimming in the Chesapeake, with the water beckoning at every turn, is practically irresistible. BUT, A WARNING: During hot summer months, the Bay is often plagued with jellyfish and nettles, whose sting is more painful than a bee's and fairly long-lasting. To some it can be dangerous. So, swim with caution; not all Bay areas are equally infested. For some visitors, the motel pool may be the better choice. The alternative, for those who enjoy surf swimming, are the ocean beaches on the Delmarva Peninsula in both states and the Atlantic shore at Virginia Beach.

FERRY RIDES AND CRUISES. Of the Chesapeake port towns that offer boat rides, the principal ones are those large enough to attract tourists in numbers or those with historical sites that are reachable only by water. In Maryland, you can find cruises from an hour to a day to a full week aboard a cruise ship. Some of the most popular are half a day long, with lunch or dinner aboard. They offer anything from a tour of harbor sights (Baltimore and Annapolis), a trip to an offshore historical site (Fort McHenry in Baltimore harbor), a sightseeing jaunt along the waterfront and backwaters (Annapolis), a trip to an offshore island (St. Clement or Smith I.), or a live-aboard, week-long cruise that takes in a vast portion of the Bay (Baltimore to Colonial Williamsburg and return). Such cruises have schedules running from just the summer months, or from April through Oct., or all year long. Many have guides who present a narrative description of the sights as you cruise. Here's a rundown of boat trips offered in Maryland waters:

Chesapeake Bay. Seven nights aboard M/V *Colonial Explorer.* Exploration Cruise Lines, 1500 Metropolitan Park Bldg., Seattle, WA 98101.

Baltimore. Six cruises from 20 min. to a full day to the 1-week trip mentioned above. (Maryland Tours, P.O. Box 47, Royal Oak, MD 21662, (301) 752–1515; or Harbor Cruises Ltd., 301 Light St., Inner Harbor, Baltimore, MD 21202, (301) 727–3113.)

Annapolis. Four cruises from 40 min. or 90 min. to 7 hrs. (Chesapeake Marine Tours, P.O. Box 3323, Annapolis, MD 21403, (301) 268–7600.)

Southern Maryland (Lower Western Shore). Three cruises: 1 hr. 40 min. from Pt. Lookout State Park to Smith I. & Rtn. (Somers Cove Marina, Crisfield, MD 21817, (301) 425–2771.) Tour boat for groups for cruises from Colton Pt. to St. Clements I. (Potomac Museum, Colton Pt., MD 20626, (301) 769–2222.) One- or 3-hr. excursions aboard a Chesapeake Bay (sailing) bugeye, with guide describing the 1814 Battle of Leonard's Creek against the British. (Calvert Marine Museum, Solomons, MD 21688, (301) 326–3719.)

Eastern Shore. 35 min. cruise across Tangier Sound to Smith I. (Capt. Jason, Box 642, Tylerton, MD 21866, (301) 425–2351.) 1-hr. 15-min. cruise to Smith I. with lunch & bus tour of Ewell, the "capital" of the island. (Somers Cove Marina, address as above.) 1-hr. cruise to Smith I. (Island Belle II, P.O. Box 12, Ewell, MD 21824, (301) 425–5431.) Narrated 1½-hr. cruise on Miles R., from Chesapeake Bay Maritime Museum at St. Michaels. (Patriot Cruises, Royal Oak, MD 21662, (301) 745–5003.) 1½-hr. cruises across Tangier Sd. to Tangier I. with box lunches available. (Steven Thomas, Crisfield, MD 21817, (301) 968–2338.) 1½-hr. cruise to Smith I. with dining at an island restaurant. (Teresa Ann Evans, c/o Skipjack Restaurant, Ewell, MD 21824, (301) 425–2201.)

Ocean City Area (Listed by boat and type of cruise). *Angler,* summer months, evening cruises of Ocean City waters; (301) 289–7424. *Bay Queen,* summer months, cruises on Assawoman Bay; (301) 289–9125. *Capt. Bunting,* summer months, cruises of Ocean City waters from the Atlantic, (301) 289–6720. *Mariner,* June–Labor Day, cruises on the Atlantic, (301) 289–9125. *Miss Ocean City,* summer months, cruises on the Atlantic, (301) 289–8234. *Starfish,* mid-July to Labor Day, evening scenic cruises on Ocean City waters, (301) 289–8547. *Taurus,* summer months, ocean cruises, (301) 289–7234.

Here are cruises in the Virginia part of the Bay:

Norfolk & Portsmouth: Boat tours (May thru Oct.) of the harbor, including the U.S. Navy Base at Norfolk and its array of warships. *Chesapeake City:* Boat tours to Lake Drummond in the Great Dismal Swamp National Wildlife Refuge. *Jamestown:* Ferry to Smith's Fort Plantation (historic site). *Smith Point:* Passenger ferries to Smith I. and Crisfield, MD. *Reedville:* Ferry to Tangier I. and on to Crisfield, MD. For information on cruise routes and schedules, write or call: Virginia Div. of Tourism, 202 N. Ninth St., Suite 500, Richmond, VA 23219, (804) 786–4484.

Small Boat Rentals. Some waterfront motels have outboard-powered skiff or daysailers (open sailboats) available for rental to their guests. Otherwise, dozens of waterfront locations all around the Bay have fishing stations that rent boats by the day or half-day. Even if you're not an angler, if you've handled an outboard boat before, a half-day rental is a fine way to get a waterside view of a place that interests you. If you have kids along, don't expect the outboard motors provided to be powerful enough to tow a waterskier. The fishing station operators usually limit rentals to 15-horsepower motors to prevent seagoing "cowboys" from damaging the boats.

Boat-Launching Ramps. For visitors intent on spending a good deal of time on the bay, for fishing or exploring, and who bring along their own boat and motor on a trailer there are literally hundreds of public launching ramps around the Bay.

Charter Fishing Boats. For those attracted by ocean fishing, over on the Delmarva Peninsula facing the Atlantic, there are "head" boats (up to 30 fishermen) and "charter" boats (up to 6) operating out of the major coastal towns. The cost ranges from about $13 (half day) to $20 (full day) for the head boats, and the most popular places are: *Maryland*—Chesapeake Beach, Ridge, and Ocean City. *Virginia*—Chincoteague, Wachapreague, Sanford, Quinby, and Cape Charles on the Delmarva Peninsula, and Little Creek, Lynnhaven, and Rudee Inlet on the Norfolk side of the Bay.

PARKS AND FORESTS. Both states are heavily dotted with state parks, forests, and both public and private campgrounds. If you are planning a family vacation with a trailer, camper, or RV, you will find dozens of camping sites on or near the Bay. For detailed information about parks and campsites, write or call as follows: *Maryland*—Office of Tourist Development, 45 Calvert St., Annapolis, MD 21401, (301) 269–3517. *Virginia*—Div. of Parks & Recreation, 1201 Washington Bldg., Capitol Sq., Richmond, VA 23219 (804) 786–2134. NOTE: *Early* reservations are *essential.*

In all, Virginia has 23 recreational and 6 historical state parks, and 6 natural areas, plus 32 private campgrounds in the Tidewater and Eastern Shore area.

Maryland lists 18 state parks and 27 private campgrounds in the Annapolis, Southern, Eastern Shore and Ocean City areas.

CANOEING. Both states, with all their rivers flowing into the Chesapeake, offer a full range of challenge to the canoeist—novice, intermediate, and expert. The Western Shore offers the most opportunities, especially on Virginia rivers—the Potomac, Rappahannock, York, and James. The visitor can choose a river and a time of year to match his skills with the degree of challenge he wants to confront. Rivers are highest and swiftest in the early spring during the winter runoff. Both states offer detailed information, including sources of canoe rental, as follows: "Virginia—A Great Place to Canoe" (pamphlet) from Div. of Tourism, Bell Tower on Capitol Sq., 101 N. Ninth St., Richmond, VA 23219, (804) 786–4484. In Maryland, the principal canoeing rivers are the Choptank and Marshyhope Rivers, and Tuckahoe Creek. Request canoeing information from: Office of Tourist Development, 45 Calvert St., Annapolis, MD 21401, (301) 269–3517.

FISHING. As of Jan. 1, 1985, a license was required to fish in the Maryland waters of the Chesapeake. A license may be purchased from: Dept. of Natural Resources, P.O. Box 1869, Annapolis, MD 21404, (301) 269–3211. Or, you may get your license at a sporting goods store when you reach the Bay. A typical cost is $7 for a 1-week tourist license.

No license is required for fishing in Virginia waters of the Bay, but one is mandatory for fishing freshwater streams and rivers.

In Maryland waters, these are the principal catches: black drum (Tangier Sd., mid-May to mid-June, and off Tilghman I., mid-June to late Aug.); red drum or channel bass (Tangier Sd., same season as above); flounder (Tangier Sd., entire summer); bluefish (entire Bay, Apr. through Dec.); also, white perch, weakfish, croaker, and trout; largemouth bass (1–3 lbs., in the Eastern Shore's tidewater rivers—Choptank, Nanticoke, Pocomoke, and Wicomico).

Virginia lists 32 species to lure the angler—18 in the Bay and 15 in the ocean. The Bay varieties include: black drum, channel bass, cobia, tarpon, striped bass, speckled trout, croaker, spot, weakfish, flounder, spadefish, and porgy; and in the Atlantic, sheepshead, tautog, sea bass, bluefish, sailfish, blue and white marlin, tuna, wahoo, king mackerel, dolphin, false albacore, amberjack, and swordfish.

In addition to its wide variety of fish, Virginia has a special enticement for visiting anglers. Each year the state conducts a Salt Water Fishing Tournament, which runs from May 1 through Nov. 30 (no charge), which awards 3,500 Citation wall plaques for catches meeting minimum tournament standards. Details for qualification are available at all harbors.

YACHT CHARTERING. If you're bound for the Chesapeake with a principal aim of chartering a sail or power yacht, perhaps for your entire vacation, but have never done so before, here is some useful information: 1) There are several ways to charter (rent) a yacht: "bareboat" (just you and your crew aboard); with captain; or, with captain *and* crew. Naturally, with captain and crew, there must be berths for all, which suggests a fairly large boat and higher charter fee. Consider the extra cost as you make your plans. 2) You must be an experienced sailor to take out a yacht—power or sail—and charterers will check you out thoroughly before they give you a yacht. Some charter operations also offer sailing lessons, so if you have *some* experience, you may be able to take lessons for a few days until you qualify to take out the yacht alone. Or you may sail with a captain for a few days, until he feels you are qualified, then put him ashore and continue the cruise alone. 3) Make sure the yacht is covered by an insurance policy providing thorough coverage for the responsibility you are assuming. Remember, if you damage or sink the boat, you're responsible; an insurance policy is your only protection. 4) The yacht will be "fully" equipped when you depart on a bareboat charter—from sailing rig and deck equipment to the last teaspoon in the galley—and you will have to sign for this inventory. Make sure you *see* every item on the list with someone from the operation *before* you sign for all of it. The list will be checked again on your return and you'll be responsible for any missing items. 5) In addition to the yacht's charter fee, you'll have to pay a "security deposit" (cash, certified check, or in some cases a credit card). These deposits vary in amount, depending on the size of yacht and amount of charter fee, but $400 is about right for a boat of 30–35 feet. Naturally, this is all returnable if there is no damage or loss. 6) Sizes of yachts available: There's no way to pin this down exactly, as different outfits use boats made by different builders. But a good range is 25 to 45 feet, suitable for 2 to 6 persons. 7) Cost: Weekly charter fees, for the boat (regardless of how many will be aboard) range between $375 and $1450, depending on size of boat. The fee for a 30-ft. sailboat (bareboat) is about $600. A captain aboard a boat will add about $125 a day. 8) *Make your arrangements well in advance* to insure getting the boat you want and out of the starting port you have chosen. The prime chartering period is mid-May through Oct. (See the list below for representative charter operations.) 9) Lay out a "rough" itinerary of Chesapeake ports you'd like to visit *before you go,* and do this with charts purchased at home from your local U.S. Government chart outlet; charts *are* available in the Bay area, of course, but sometimes summer demand causes marinas to run out of the one you need and you'll waste time chasing around to find it. 10) For a complete guide to charter operations in the Chesapeake, write to: Chesapeake Bay Yacht Charter Assn., P.O. Box 4022, Annapolis, MD 21403, and request their brochure listing member companies. 11) To get a sweeping sense of all you can see and do while sailing, you may want to purchase "Guide to Cruising Chesapeake Bay," available at $19.95 (plus $1.50 postage) from: Chesapeake Bay Magazine, 1819 Bay Ridge Ave., Suite 200, Annapolis, MD 21403. You can order by phone, too, (301) 263–2662, charging the guide to your VISA or MasterCard.

Most of the yacht charter operations listed below will send detailed information on boats available, accommodations, charter rates, deposits, insurance, experience requirements, and sailing lessons if offered. All firms listed below offer sailboats exclusively, unless otherwise indicated:

The Sailing Emporium, Green Lane, Rock Hall, MD 21661, (301) 778–1342; *Gratitude Boat Charters,* Lawton Ave., Rock Hall, MD 21661 (301) 639–7111; *Pelorus Yacht Sales,* Rt. 1, Bayside Ave., Rock Hall, MD 21661, (301) 639–7377; *Kendall's Marina,* S. Walnut St., Rock Hall, MD 21661, (301) 639–7177; *La Vida Yacht Charters,* Rt. 2, Box 759E, Chestertown, MD 21620, (301) 778–6330; *North East-Wind Yacht Charter,* 326 First St., Annapolis, MD 21403, (800) 638–5139; *Dockside Charter Services,* 326 First St., Annapolis, MD 21403, (800) 638–4300; *Nauticat Motorsailers,* 222 Severn Ave., Annapolis, MD 21403, (301) 268–9005; *Chesapeake Yacht Charters,* 1700 Bowleys Quarters Rd., Baltimore, MD 21220, (301) 335–6677; *Tradewind Charters, Inc.,* 2 E. Fayette St., Baltimore, MD 21202, (301) 467–7788; *Yachting Vacations,* 1402 Colony Rd., Pasadena, MD 21122, (301) 437–5811; *Lippencott Sailing Yachts,* Rt. 1, Box 545, Grasonville, MD 21638, (301) 827–9300; *Commonwealth Yachts,* P.O. Box 1070, Gloucester Pt., VA 23062, (804) 642–2150; *Sassafras Charters* (powerboats), 404C St. Albans Ct., Chester Springs, PA 19425, (215) 524–0196; *Huntly Yacht Charters* (power & sail), Preston Rd., Wernersville, PA 19565, (215) 678–BOAT (call collect); *Red Sky at Night,* 4407 Verona Dr., Wilmington, DE 19808; *Zahniser's,* Inc., call for charter information: (301) 326–2663.

 COLONIAL SITES. For the visitor to the Chesapeake who is also fascinated by the Colonial era in the American story, the Bay offers dozens of opportunities to see history first hand. Wander just a few miles inland from the Bay or its tributaries and you step into the center of Colonial and Revolutionary War history.

If we consider the Bay area as divided—by nature and state boundaries—into four sections, the Eastern and Western Shores of both Virginia and Maryland, the Western Shore of Virginia offers the maximum convenient opportunity to visit a range of colonial sites while focussing primarily on the Bay. What follows is a generous sampling of such sites just off the Bay, but it should be emphasized that there are historic buildings, homes, inns, military headquarters, and battle-grounds all around the rim of the Bay, though in smaller concentrations than on Virginia's Western Shore. The explanation is simple: It is here, between Norfolk and the Potomac River where the first permanent English colony was established, that many of the area's most famous plantations were begun, and that the climactic final battle of the American Revolution was fought. (It is worth noting that you have only to range a little further inland to reach the part of Virginia where dozens of Civil War battles were fought. In fact, 60 percent of *all* the battles in that war were fought on Virginia soil.)

So we begin with Virginia's Tidewater region, that stretch of shore between Norfolk and the Potomac, and pick up the start of a historic site tour:

In Norfolk itself, there's the *Hermitage Foundation Museum* (a splendid collection of Oriental objects, and a picnic ground); then the *Adam Thoroughgood House* (built in 1636, the oldest standing brick house in America); next, the *Willoughby-Baylor House* (built 1794); and finally, the *House of Moses Myers,* one of America's first millionaires, with hosts and hostesses in period costumes serving as guides.

Going north across Norfolk harbor to Hampton, you'll find the 63-acre expanse of *Fort Monroe,* a hexagonal bastion surrounded by a moat; here, over a 150-year span, distinguished prisoners such as Indian chief Black Hawk and Confederate President Jefferson Davis were incarcerated.

A bit to the northwest, in Newport News, the *Mariner's Museum* is—while not Colonial—a must-see stop for maritime/nautical buffs. The museum has the outstanding Crabtree Collection of Miniature Ships, other models, marine paintings, figureheads, and nautical memorabilia.

Driving west for 23 miles on I-64 brings you to the Colonial Parkway and the state Information Centers at Jamestown, Colonial Williamsburg, and Yorktown. In Jamestown, there's a walking tour that includes the settlement's original church tower and the foundations of many of the earliest buildings. A mile away is Jamestown Festival Park (built by the state in 1957), where the visitor can go aboard reproductions of the *Susan Constant, Godspeed,* and *Discovery,* the three tiny ships that carried the first settlers here.

In Williamsburg, 60 years of painstaking restoration (with Rockefeller family funds) has returned Virginia's second capital to a startlingly accurate reproduction of life in Colonial days; especially popular with visitors are the bakery, the print shop, the blacksmith's forge, and the wig-maker's shop. And it's fascinating to walk along the broad main thoroughfare from the magnificent capitol building at one end to the College of William and Mary at the other (America's second-oldest, founded in 1693), passing as you stroll guides, soldiers, and shopkeepers, all garbed in authentic Colonial dress.

Not far from Williamsburg—only a few minutes' drive—is *Yorktown,* where combined American and French forces, commanded by General George Washington, defeated British General Lord Cornwallis on Oct. 19, 1781, and brought a successful end to the American Revolution. At the Yorktown Information Center, you can trace the steps in this final climactic battle against the British redoubt, and see tents used by Washington's troops and a diorama of the battle.

Depending on how far inland you want to drive on State Rt. 5 toward Richmond, as it winds roughly along the James River (the total distance is 51 mi.), you can see the greatest concentration of great houses and plantations anywhere in the U.S. Six miles east of Williamsburg (on Rt. 60) is *Carter's Grove,* a 1750 mansion built by wealthy Robert "King" Carter, whose home is considered one of the most beautiful in America. At Jamestown, you can take a ferry across the James to *Smith's Fort Plantation,* and see the foundations of the breastworks built in 1609 by Capt. John Smith. On these grounds is the *Rolfe-Warren House,* a brick structure built in 1652.

Moving west from Williamsburg, you encounter a procession of famous colonial homes. First is *Sherwood Forest,* built by President John Tyler, who fancied himself a "political Robin Hood." Then comes *Bel Air,* built in 1670, one of the oldest frame dwellings in the country. Following that is *Evelynton,* a white-columned mansion built by the ancestors of the Byrds of Virginia. (You may visit Bel Air by appointment only; Evelynton is closed to the public.) The great William Byrd II himself—diarist, member of the Colonial governor's council, explorer, and founder of Richmond—once owned 179,000 acres of Virginia land and lived nearby in *Westover.*

Next in the sequence is *Berkeley,* the ancestral home of Col. Benjamin Harrison, a signer of the Declaration of Independence and later, president. Last in the series along Rt. 5 is *Shirley Plantation,* a home that has been in the Hill-Carter family for nine generations, since 1723. This was the home of Robert E. Lee's mother, Anne Hill Carter, and it still contains many of the original furnishings.

The section of Virginia lying between the Rappahannock and Potomac Rivers is renowned for producing U.S. presidents and statesmen. In this area, King George County gave us President James Madison, and Westmoreland County was the birthplace of George Washington, James Monroe, and Robert E. Lee. The Lee house, *Stratford Hall,* was started in 1725 by Thomas Lee. All told, this home produced 12 members of the Virginia House of Burgesses, four governors, the Revolution's Light Horse Harry Lee (Washington's cavalry commander), and the Confederacy's Robert E. Lee. Stratford Hall was built of brick shipped from England, in the shape of a capital H. It measures 60 by 90 feet. Its 1,500 acres are still worked as they were in Colonial times. The house overlooks the Potomac, only 8 miles from Wakefield, the birthplace of George Washington.

Wakefield is an approximation of Washington's home (the original burned down on Christmas Day, 1779), and was rebuilt by the National Park Service. Many of the original furnishings were saved and may be seen at Wakefield.

For those willing to wander further, or for those approaching from the west, Virginia has *many* more fascinating colonial sites. South of Appomattox (west of Petersburg on US 460) lies *Red Hill Shrine,* the home of the great patriot Patrick Henry. *Staunton* (I-65, NW of Richmond) is the family home of President Woodrow Wilson, and near Leesburg (NW of Washington, D.C., on Rt. 7) is *Oatlands Plantation,* a classical revival mansion built in 1800 by George Carter, the great-grandson of "King" Carter, whose mansion is near Williamsburg. The bricks and lumber for this great home were produced on this 3,400-acre plantation, and the terraced formal gardens are among the finest examples of early Virginia landscape design. Also near Leesburg is *Morven Park,* with a mile-long tree-lined drive leading to the house, the former home of Gov. Westmoreland Davis, with its Greek revival portico, a Jacobean dining room, a French drawing room and a library. The house is furnished with intricately carved furniture, oriental rugs, 16th Century tapestries, and rare porcelain, china, and silverware.

As you circle the Bay, visiting the places that attract you the most, dozens of signs, historical markers on highways, and Maryland and Virginia highway information centers will lie along your wandering route. Each will help guide you to historical sites that span over 350 years of America's past. You won't be bored around Chesapeake Bay, but you may have a problem finding enough time to see all the sights and do all the things that are waiting there for you.

THE CHESAPEAKE

THE CHESAPEAKE

Maryland and Virginia's Watery Vacationland

by
JAMES LOUTTIT

It all started when the Atlantic drowned the Susquehanna.

If that sounds macabre, don't worry about it; geologically speaking, it wasn't a particularly violent affair. In fact, the Chesapeake's proud residents and millions of annual visitors to this watery vacationland would call the drowning justifiable.

Ten thousand years ago, give or take a few centuries, there was no Bay. Starting somewhere in the mountains to the north, there was only the river, flowing cold and gently south to the sea. Melting glaciers changed all that. Slowly, inexorably, rising ocean tidal waters drowned the lower reaches of the river and formed what is today the major inlet

37

on the Eastern Seaboard—a great shallow filigree of a bay that is almost 200 miles long but seldom more than 20 miles wide. The Susquehanna now flows *into* the Bay, as do some 45 other rivers and streams. These include (to name but a few) Virginia's Rappahannock, York, and James in the south, Maryland's Patuxent, Choptank, Chester, and Sassafras in the north, and the mighty Potomac in between. Combined, they and their lesser sisters join the Atlantic to form America's largest estuary— a gentle blending of fresh river and salty sea that spreads over 3,277 square miles, has an average depth of 21 feet, and embraces a tidal shoreline of almost 6,000 miles.

The Chesapeake Vacationland begins at the water's edge, and all that is most important to the Bay is but a few short miles from its shores. Visitors have recognized this happy fact since this great bay was formed some ten thousand years ago.

About 8000 B.C. or So

The first tourists to the Chesapeake were probably Midwesterners— nomadic Indian deer hunters who drifted in when the Susquehanna was still giving ground to the Bay. This may have been as early as 8,000 B.C.; they were certainly there four thousand years later. Not too surprising, they liked what they saw—and they stayed. These Stone Age travelers, with their straight black hair, dark eyes, and red-brown skin, were the descendants of earlier prehistory wanderers who had migrated eastward across the Bering Strait "bridge" more than 20 thousand years before, spreading slowly to the south and then eastward across the Great Plains. Their descendants, in turn, later became the Powhatan Confederacy, a scattered group of some 30 Eastern Woodlands tribes whose loose "family" tie was the Algonquian language. (Other than the common thread of language, there is little evidence that they liked each other very much—and there is *no* evidence they wanted anything to do with those English-speaking strangers who would someday move into the Bay.)

The Powhatan, in time, were comfortably ensconced in some 200 palisaded villages along coastal Virginia and around the shores of Chesapeake Bay. Now out of the Stone Age, they still hunted rabbits and deer in the woodlands, but now they also raised corn and enjoyed the bountiful fruits of their bay-front homes—the fish, crabs, and oysters that would someday make the Chesapeake famous. This was the Good Life: a mild climate, plenty to eat, and only an occasional tribal squabble to keep the juices flowing. But like all things, good or bad, it was bound to change; somewhere beyond the eastern horizon a new breed of adventurer was beginning to eye the Powhatan's watery paradise.

1492 and All That

Columbus, we know, sailed westward from Spain in 1492 and discovered America. Then, for the next few centuries, Spanish soldiers, priests, and adventurers busied themselves in South and Central America (and even in Florida, Texas, New Mexico, and California), converting the natives, looking for gold, and reintroducing the horse to the place the horse had started but was now totally extinct. Spain's influence in the New World was enormous, but her adventurers sometimes neglected or ignored some of the better touring places—the Chesapeake, for example. It took a ragtag crew of Englishmen to capitalize on this oversight.

The British Are Coming

Spaniards visited the Chesapeake in the early 1500s, and Giovanni de Verrazano, sailing for France, probably sailed into the bay in 1524 on his way north to New York Harbor, but the bay remained relatively peaceful through most of that century. Although English seadogs Drake, Gilbert, and Raleigh were harassing Spanish shipping in the Americas, the British Crown gave little serious thought to New World colonization until her captains had smashed the Spanish Armada in 1588. Two feeble attempts had been made a few years before, but each had been a failure.

The first attempt by Englishmen to settle in the New World was made in 1585, when Sir Walter dispatched a small band of settlers westward across the Atlantic. Those first English colonists landed on Roanoke Island between North Carolina's Albermarle and Pamlico Sounds. They sailed home to England in 1586. A second group tried again in the same place the following year, but they had disappeared without a trace when the busy folks back home finally got around to sending them supplies in 1591. That second desperate little band has gone down in history as a sad footnote: The Lost Colony of Roanoke.

True to character, the British tried again, this time landing further north at Jamestown (Virginia), near the entrance to the great Bay. It was anything but roses, but this third colony survived. Established May 14, 1607, by the London Company, this first *permanent* English settlement on a peninsula (now an island) in the James River fought disease, starvation, and hostile Indians until supplies and more settlers finally arrived. Seven months after the original 105 settlers landed, only 32 were still alive. Baron Thomas West De la Warr (note *that* name) arrived in 1610 and persuaded Jamestown's surviving colonists to hang on. It's hard to imagine exactly what De la Warr said to convince them that things could possibly be worse back in England, but the good baron prevailed—the colonists stayed and the colony did indeed survive. One of America's first states (the *first* of the original 13 colonies to ratify the Constitution) now bears De la Warr's name.

If it was Baron De la Warr who finally persuaded those early colonists to remain, it was tough-minded Captain John Smith who kept them going during the "starveing tyme" between 1607 and 1609. And, believe it or not, that celebrated story of Smith's capture by Chief Powhatan (Wahunsonacock) and his rescue by the chief's daughter, Pocahontas, is probably true. John Rolfe, who began cultivating tobacco in Virginia in 1612, helped ensure the struggling colony's survival when he married Pocahontas in 1614 and took his Indian bride back to England two years later. The Smith–Pocahontas–Rolfe triangle is yet another intriguing fragment of early American history, and one can't help but wonder if an Indian princess, not Martha Washington, wasn't truly America's *first* First Lady?

Captain Smith was a busy fellow during those early years of the Virginia Colony—cajoling his dispirited fellow colonists not to lose hope and prodding them when they did, but also finding time to explore the great Bay to the north in 1608. Smith charted the Bay and wrote colorful descriptions of what he saw, but it was another strong-willed Englishman, William Claiborne, who became the first European to settle in present-day Maryland. Claiborne, also of Virginia, established a fur-trading post on Kent Island in the Upper Bay in 1631. (The Chesapeake Bay Bridge, US 50, today crosses over Kent Island, linking Maryland's Western and Eastern Shores.)

In 1632, King Charles I of England gave the whole region to George Calvert, the first Lord Baltimore, but George died before the king signed the charter. It was then chartered to George's son, Cecil, the second Lord Baltimore. These chartered lands were named "Maryland" in honor of Queen Henrietta Maria, wife of King Charles.

The first Maryland colonists arrived two years later (1634) aboard two small ships, *Ark* and *Dove.* They landed on St. Clements Island in the Potomac on the western shore, not far down the Bay from Claiborne's Kent Island trading post. The new colonists established St. Maries Citty (St. Mary's City in St. Mary's County). Although Claiborne's settlement was now part of the colony, the doughty trader refused to accept Lord Baltimore's authority. In 1654, five years after the colony passed a religious toleration act, Claiborne seized control. He held onto the colony for four years, but the crown prevailed and Claiborne returned Maryland to Lord Baltimore in 1658. A Protestant group led by John Coode took over in 1689, demanding that England take control of the government, which it did in 1691.

What those original Algonquin inhabitants thought of all this isn't hard to imagine. Most soon decided the old neighborhood wasn't what it used to be, packed up, and moved out, leaving little behind but some of their tribal names—Patuxent, Choptank, Portobago, Wicomico, and others.

Three "Home" Wars

The American Revolution, the War of 1812, and the Civil War all touched the Chesapeake—sometimes lightly, often with hammer blows. A great natural bay, with its rivers and harbors, it is a magnet for the peaceful—and for the aggressive. The same attributes that attracted its first settlers, Indian or European, made the Chesapeake a natural target in times of war.

Neither state has a monopoly on historic sites from America's first three "home" wars. If the last decisive battle of the Revolution was fought at Yorktown, Virginia in 1781, one of the first cargoes of British tea was burned with the British ship *Peggy Stewart* in Annapolis harbor in 1774.

The British returned to the Chesapeake in 1814, during the War of 1812, winning early victories against England's former colonies. British troops eventually burned the young nation's Capitol and White House in Washington, but they later suffered a major defeat at Fort McHenry near Baltimore. Neither side had much heart for the war after that.

Although both Virginia and Maryland were slave states, the two found themselves on opposite sides during the Civil War, 1861–1865. After Virginia joined the Confederacy, the fate of Washington, D.C. depended on whether Maryland remained in the Union. It finally did, although many Marylanders fought for the Confederacy. Many of the biggest and the bloodiest battles of the war took place in Virginia, but several major campaigns were fought in Maryland. The first duel between two ironclads, the *Monitor* and the *Merrimac,* was fought to a draw in Chesapeake Bay off Newport News, Virginia. Battle sites, museums, and historic monuments from each of these three wars are discussed in greater detail in later chapters.

The Chesapeake Today

Change is inevitable, and there have been changes, but much of the Bay and its surrounding tidal lands remain as they were three or four hundred years ago.

Thousands of miles of natural woodland still fringe the Bay, forests and scrub pines spreading outwards from the low-lying shores. Great reaches of Chesapeake Bay are much the same as Captain Smith saw it in 1608, disturbed only by an occasional reminder that this *is* the 20th Century and change *is* inevitable.

In the Upper Bay, Baltimore rises proudly above its rejuvenated Inner Harbor, a happy reminder of the way things were and what they can be; while in the south, near the wide mouth of the great Bay, Norfolk strives to blend in harmony our past, our present, and our future.

Two great bridges now span the Bay, engineering marvels that would have sent Captain Smith reeling. In the north, near Annapolis, the twin graceful arches of the William Preston Lane, Jr. Memorial Bridge link Maryland's Eastern and Western shores; while in the south, near the ocean entrance to the Bay, the Chesapeake Bay Bridge and Tunnel complex ties Norfolk's Cape Henry with Delmarva's Cape Charles.

Along the middle reaches of the Chesapeake, where Maryland's Calvert Cliffs Nuclear Plant is a modern symbol of the Atomic Age, dozens of quiet hamlets and small backwater ports still look much as they did centuries ago. The past and the present are usually at peace with each other in the Chesapeake—and this, as much as anything, bodes well for our future and the future of the Bay.

Chesapeake Weather

Few things are perfect; few *places* are perfect. So, face it—Chesapeake weather is good, but it's not perfect.

That inveterate traveler, Captain John Smith, described it this way:

"The sommer is hot as in Spaine. The winter colde as in France or England. The heat of sommer is in June, July, and August, but commonly the coole breeses assuage the vehemencie of the heat."

In other words, translating from Smith's Olde English: Neither a tiger, nor a pussycat.

Smith was right; "the heat of sommer" is indeed in June, July, and August. The Chesapeake has a long summer season, at least a month longer on either end than neighboring areas to the north. The "normal" temperature in Baltimore, in the Upper Bay, ranges from 54.2 (degrees Fahrenheit) in April, to an average high of 76.8 in July, and back to 57 in October. Norfolk, at the lower end of the Bay, has "normal" averages of 58 in April, 78.8 in July, and 62 in October.

Smith was also right about those "coole breeses." The breezes are generally southerly (that is, they head south) during a Chesapeake summer. Calms are frequent, especially at night and in the morning. In early summer, and again in the fall, winds usually blow up or down the Bay. Rainfall is relatively light during those early and late-season months. It is heaviest in June, July, and August, when occasional violent thunderstorms shatter the midsummer calms.

Captain Smith described a brief but blustery early-summer Chesapeake thundersquall as "an extreme gust of wind, raine, thunder and lightning (and) with great danger we escaped the unmerciful raging of that ocean-like water."

"Wind, raine, thunder and lightning"—guaranteed to earn your respect, and useful for cooling things off. The good captain knew what he was talking about. Chesapeake Bay thundersqualls are legendary, but they seldom last long, and they do "assuage the vehemencie of the heat."

There is very little fog during a Chesapeake summer, but those long clear hot spells encourage a variety of unpleasant critters—especially sea nettles (poisonous jellyfish) and mosquitoes. Nettles can be a real nuisance in warm, quiet waters, while mosquitoes are likely to be found (actually, *they* find *you*) where the land is marshy and when the weather is damp. Mosquitoes are likely to be thickest in early summer, especially in the marshlands below the Choptank on Maryland's Eastern Shore.

On the other side of the coin, the Chesapeake's unique blending of fresh and salt water, and its temperate location between the colder north and the hotter south, make the Bay a near-perfect breeding or nesting home for a wide variety of fish and fowl—and a mecca for anglers and hunters. Half a million geese invade the fields and wet lands of the Eastern Shore during the peak of the Canadian migration. And last but not least of the Chesapeake's native—and famous—inhabitants are its shellfish. If the Oyster is King of the Chesapeake, the Crab is its Prime Minister. They need the Bay's perfectly proportioned waters, and the Bay needs them; neither would be the same without the other.

Perhaps it's not perfect, but the waters and surrounding tidelands of Chesapeake Bay are a unique tourist magnet. Easily reached and easily explored, the Chesapeake Vacationland has something for everyone—major cities and tiny villages, ocean beaches and quiet backwaters, "theme" parks and historic sites, and an abundance of wonderful food, from Maryland crab to Virginia ham.

Amy Harold

MARYLAND'S WESTERN SHORE

Three Southern Counties—Calvert, Charles, and St. Mary's

Maryland was born on these gentle shores.

The date was March 25, 1634; the place St. Clement's Island in the Potomac, just off Colton Point.

The Indians were there first, but their lease was running out. John Smith inspected the property in 1608, but the captain had a lot of things on his mind and didn't stay very long. William Claiborne had staked a claim to a nice piece of bay-front property on Kent Island in 1631. He was still there when the first Maryland colonists landed from *Ark* and *Dove* three years later. Claiborne fixed the newcomers with a jaundiced eye, not sure that he didn't prefer the Powhatans to his new neighbors from England. Trader Claiborne stuck around long enough to become a royal pain in the breeches to his king and to Lord Baltimore, but that's another story.

The new arrivals were also in Maryland to stay. Devout Catholics, they first erected a cross on St. Clement's Island, then built a small fort—a "pallizado of one hundred and twentie yards square"—a short distance away. Within a short time settlers had scattered over several miles of the peninsula between the Chesapeake and the Potomac, and had founded St. Maries Citty, which would be Maryland's colonial capital for 60 years. Historic St. Mary's City today features an interpretive museum and visitor center, a reconstruction of Maryland's first state house, archaeological digs, and living-history exhibits.

Tucked away between bay and river, Maryland's most historic region is all-too-often its forgotten shore, but Southern Marylanders are proud of their roots and they are changing that; there are more touring attractions in the area each year. Especially noteworty is *Maryland Dove,* a replica of Lord Baltimore's square-rigged *Dove,* which is docked on St. Mary's River, St. Mary's City.

Maryland's three Southern Counties, plus adjacent St. George's, are a quiet, sparsely populated land of tobacco fields, 18th-Century towns, and stately tidewater plantations. The region is also a gastronomical delight, for this is also the natural home of the oyster and crab and Southern Maryland stuffed ham. Southern Maryland celebrates its tobacco crop—the early cavaliers' "green gold"—each spring, March till May, when the warehouses in La Plata, Hughesville, and Waldorf are crowded with buyers, sellers, and tourists and ring with the singsong chant of tobacco auctioneers; its history during the Patuxent River Appreciation Days (October); the succulent oyster during St. Mary's County Oyster Festival (also October); its heritage at the "No Foolin" Antiques Show in March, and the crab year round.

Southern Maryland—on the Bay's Western Shore—should be enjoyed at your leisure, but be prepared to let your belt out at least one notch, two for a longer stay.

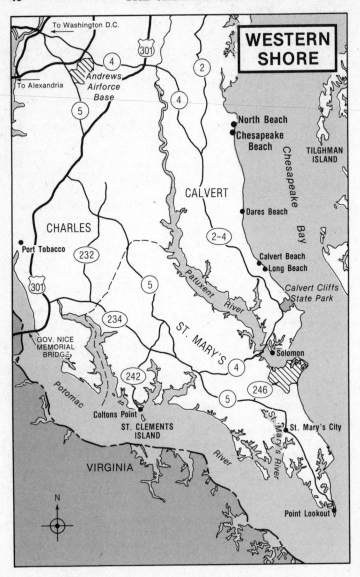

PRACTICAL INFORMATION FOR MARYLAND'S WESTERN SHORE

PLACES TO STAY

 MOTELS AND INNS. Maryland's three southern counties—Calvert, Charles, and St. Mary's—are a rural area of the Western Shore, with numerous small towns and hamlets but no major urban centers. Although there are many small motels throughout the region, there are few major motel complexes complete with full-line restaurants. The following is a selection only of those that are available.

Calvert County

Lexington Park Motor Lodge. *Inexpensive.* 97 Coral Dr., 20653; 863–9411. 28 motel units, with restaurant nearby. MC, V.

Bowen's Inn. *Inexpensive to Moderate.* P.O. Box 35, Solomons, 20688; 326–2214. Nine hotel units, with marina and restaurant nearby.

Island Manor Motel. *Inexpensive.* 1 Main St., Solomons Island, 20688; 326–3700. 10 motel units, with restaurant. AE, MC, V.

Charles County

Bel Alton Motel. *Inexpensive.* US 301, 20611; 934–9505 or 8331. 29 motel units, with restaurant nearby. Outdoor pool. MC, V.

Lafayette Motel. *Inexpensive.* US 301, Bel Alton, 20611; 934–8233. 38 motel units, with a restaurant nearby. MC, V.

Econo Lodge. *Inexpensive.* US 301 and Rt. 6, La Plata, 20646; 934–8196 or (800) 446–6900. 60 units. Pool, Continental breakfasts. Restaurant nearby. AE, MC, V.

La Plata Motel. *Inexpensive.* P.O. Box 666, 20646; 934–8121 or 8122. 40 motel units, restaurant nearby. AE, MC, V.

Heidelberg Motel Venture. *Inexpensive.* US 301, Waldorf, 645–5683. 30 motel units, restaurant nearby. AE, MC, V.

Holiday Inn of Waldorf. *Inexpensive to Moderate.* US 301 and St. Patrick's Dr., 20601; 645–8200 or 800 HOLIDAY. 193 units in a three-story motel. Pool, restaurant, and bar. AE, CB, DC, MC, V.

St. Mary's County

Village Motel. *Inexpensive.* Rt. 5, Box 92, Charlotte Hall, 20622; 884–3172. 32 units. Outdoor pool. Restaurant nearby. MC, V.

Leonardtown Motel. *Inexpensive.* 25 W. Park Ave., Leonardtown, 20650; 475–5650. 25 motel units. MC, V.

Belvedere Motor Inn. *Inexpensive to Moderate.* 60 Main St., Lexington Park, 20653; 863–6666. 166 units, including efficiencies. Outdoor pool, restaurant, with tennis nearby. AE, DC, MC, V.

Patuxent Inn. *Moderate.* P.O. Box 778, Lexington Park, 20653; 862–4100. 120 hotel rooms, with outdoor pool, restaurant, and meeting rooms. Tennis and golf packages. AE, MC, V.

Lord Calvert Motel. *Inexpensive.* Rt. 235, Lexington Park, 20653; 863–8131. 29 motel units, with outdoor pool. Restaurant nearby. MC, V.

PLACES TO EAT

RESTAURANTS. The emphasis as a general rule is on good food, not decor, in Calvert, Charles, and St. Mary's Counties. And, still as a general rule, that good food will be fresh from the Bay or nearby farms. This is the Land of the Oyster and Crab, and few will complain about that. The following is of course a selection only of the numerous seafood and general restaurants that dot the area, especially near the Bay.

Calvert County

Soloman's Crabhouse. *Moderate.* Rts. 2 and 4, Solomons, 20688; 326–2800. Open year round, seven days a week, 11 A.M. to 10 P.M. Spicy Maryland steamed crabs and every other way. The Crabhouse is an old firehouse with a nice harbor view.

Charles County

Harbor View Inn. *Moderate.* Route 243, Compton, 475–9432. Steamed crabs with country music and a view of Combs Creek. The inn is open year round, 11 A.M. to midnight. Eat in or carry out.

St. Mary's County

Evan's Crab House. *Moderate.* St. George's Island; 994–2299. Hard shell crab and soft shell crab sandwiches. Open all year, closed Mondays, 4 P.M. to 11 P.M. weekdays, from noon till 11 P.M. weekends. Dockage available on St. George's Creek.

Duffy's Tavern. *Inexpensive to Moderate.* Scotland Beach on the Chesapeake; 872–4001. Open mid-April till mid-November, Duffy's eat-in, carry-out features steamed crabs and Duffy's Crab Soup. A good view of the Bay.

Farthing's Ordinary. *Moderate to Expensive.* A reconstructed 17th-Century inn, with outbuildings, open for dining. (See Historic St. Mary's City under "Things to See and Do.") 862–9880.

THINGS TO SEE AND DO

Calvert County

Battle Creek Cypress Swamp Sanctuary. One of the northernmost stands of bald cypress in America, the swamp is located on Grays Rd., off Rt. 506. Self-guided elevated tours. Open 10 A.M. to 5 P.M. Tuesday through Saturday, 1 P.M. to 5 P.M. Sunday. Visitors center (535–5327).

Calvert Cliffs State Park. Rts. 2 and 4, south of Lusby. Thirty miles of the Chesapeake's western shore, first described by Captain Smith. Famous for its Miocene fossils, 15 to 30 million years old. Scavenging permitted but no digging allowed on cliffs. Open March through October, sunrise to sunset. 326–4728.

Calvert Cliffs Nuclear Power Plant Museum. Rts. 2 and 4, Lusby. Dioramas and exhibits in a converted tobacco barn. Open 9 A.M. to 5 P.M., closed Christmas. 234–7484. Free.

Calvert Marine Museum. Rt. 2, Solomons Local maritime history and fossils from Calvert Cliffs. Drum Point Lighthouse and cruises on a converted 1899 bugeye, *Wm. B. Tennison.* Open daily. 326–3719. Donations accepted. During the fall and winter, September through March, visitors can see working oyster boats at Broomes Island, Chesapeake Beach, and Solomons Island.

Chesapeake Beach Railway Museum. Rt. 261, Chesapeake Beach. Housed in old railway station; exhibits depicting 1890s resort. Sunday, 1 to 4 P.M. Free.

Cove Point Light Station. Cove Point Rd., Rt. 497, off Rts. 2 and 4, Cove Point. Oldest lighthouse on the Bay, with a great view of the Chesapeake and Calvert Cliffs. 326–3254. Free.

Jefferson Patterson Park and Museum. 52 archaeological sites on 2½ miles of Patuxent River shoreline. Located on Mackall Rd. (Rt. 265), Port Republic. Location of Battle of St. Leonard's Creek, largest naval engagement in Maryland waters during War of 1812. Museum and visitors center. Open summers, Wednesday through Sunday. Donations.

Charles County

Dr. Mudd's House. Back a fair piece from the water, but an interesting side trip, Dr. Samuel A. Mudd's restored farm home is on Rt. 232, Bryantown. Dr. Mudd's descendants will show you where the unlucky doctor set John Wilkes Booth's broken leg after the actor had shot President Lincoln. Open weekends, April till late November. 884–3717 or 934–8464. Admission.

1819 Charles County Courthouse. A reconstructed Federal courthouse in Port Tobacco, with tobacco and archaeological exhibits. Closed January and February. 934–4313. Admission.

Historic Port Tobacco. Rts. 6 and 427, several miles west of US 301, Port Tobacco is the site of the first permanent English settlement in Charles County. Historic Federal-style courthouse (Chapel Point Rd.) and museum, 10 till 4, Wednesday through Saturday, and at noon Sunday, June through August;

Saturday and Sunday only April–May, September–December. Closed January–March. 934–4313. Admission.

Tobacco Auctions. La Plata, Waldorf, and Hughesville, mid-March through the first week in May. Open Monday through Thursday, 9 A.M. until the last leaf's sold. 645–2693. Free.

Smallwood's Retreat. This restored Colonial tidewater plantation is located in Smallwood State Park, Rison, quite a way up the Potomac from the Bay. Outbuildings illustrate 18th-Century plantation life. House open weekends. 743–7613. Free.

St. Mary's County

Cecil's Mill. This three-story mill and country store in Great Mills (Rt. 471) houses a crafts shop, where some 90 artisans demonstrate and sell local arts and handicrafts. Open mid-March till November. Closed Thanksgiving. 994–1510 or 1770.

Chancellor's Point Natural History Area. St. Mary's City. Sixty-six acres of woodland, marsh, beach, and bluff on St. Mary's River. Open daily except Christmas, sunrise to sunset.

Godiah Spray Tobacco Plantation. St. Mary's City. This is a working reconstruction of a 17th-Century tobacco farm. Living history presentations during the summer. The plantation is part of Historic St. Mary's City (see below). 862–9880 or 1661. Admission.

Historic St. Mary's City. An outdoor history museum on 800 acres on the site of Maryland's first settlement and first capital. The museum's visitors center is housed in a complex of restored farm houses (862–9880) and includes information, a gift shop, and exhibits. Other Historic St. Mary's City features are State House of 1676, *Maryland Dove*, Godiah Spray Tobacco Plantation, Chancellor's Point Natural History Center, and Farthing's Ordinary inn. This focal point of early Maryland history is open from noon to 4 P.M. weekends from January through mid-March; 10:30 to 4, October through December and mid-March through May, Wednesday through Sunday; and daily, 10 till 5 during the summer season, June through September. 862–9880. Admission.

Point Lookout State Park and Fort Lincoln. Civil War exhibits at the visitors center (Rt. 5) and the Point Lookout Confederate Cementary, where prisoners were interred. The earthen fort was built by Confederate POWs. Open daily except Thanksgiving and Christmas week. 872–5688. Free.

St. Clement's Island. Off Colton Point, Rt. 242. A 40-foot cross—not the original!—marks the spot the first settlers landed from *Ark* and *Dove* in 1634. Boat tours available at St. Clement's Island-Potomac Museum, Thursday evenings. Reservations necessary. 762–2222. The museum on Bay View Road, Colton Point, has exhibits spanning 12,000 years. Open weekdays, 9 till 4, and weekends 12:30 to 4:30. Call during winter months, 769–2222. Donations.

Sotterley on the Patuxent. A lovely Georgian mansion and plantation (1717) off Rt. 245 near Hollywood. English country gardens. Open June through September, 11 A.M. to 5 P.M. 373–2280. Admission.

ANNAPOLIS

by
ELEANOR ELY

The Indians were there first, of course. But only occasionally. There was a nice little river and some creeks, tidal beaches for shell-gathering to make wampum, oyster beds everywhere, and a half-day's canoe trip across the Bay to visit the folks. There were so many places like it along the edge of that 200-mile bay, east side and west side, that it wasn't even bothersome when a group of white families moved in and settled on the land between the nice little rivers. After all, there had been other white settlers in patches around the Bay for at least a man's lifetime. The Indians simply moved off.

They had no realization, or much concern, that the whole area had been given to Cecil Calvert, second Baron of Baltimore. The lovely

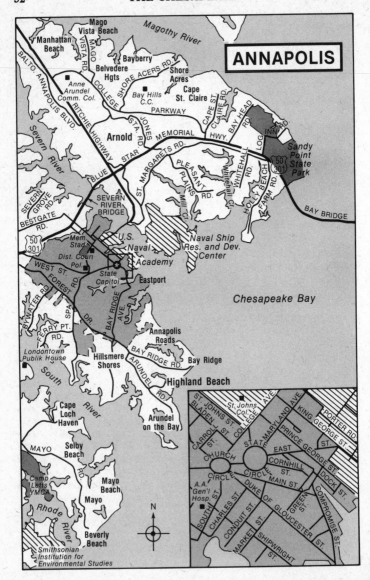

forests, beaches, and fields around the river had been given the name of Calvert's wife, Anne Arundel's County.

First settled by Puritans and called Providence, this harbor-side village prospered and grew, spreading south of the Severn River. In 20 years it became an important cargo landing place called Anne Arundel Town or Arundelton. Twenty-five years later the town became an official entry port of the colony of Maryland, and in 1695 when it became the capital of the Maryland Colony, its name was changed to Annapolis, City of Anne, daughter of William and Mary, Princess of England who later would be Queen Anne. In 1708 the town on the Severn was named a city by charter. It quickly grew into an important center for commerce and society in the colony. Maryland's first newspaper was published in Annapolis in 1745.

The Maryland State House was built in 1772 and it was there that the young Congress of the United States met from November 1783 to August 1784. George Washington resigned as Commander-in-Chief of the Continental Army in the State House in December 1783, and in early 1784 Congress there signed the Treaty of Paris which ended the Revolutionary War.

Annapolis was familiar with the great and the near-great by the time Congress moved out. It settled back complacently to commerce and building and hardly turned a hair when, in 1845, the United States Naval Academy was founded on the Severn to "create a select group of gentlemen and scholar officers." After all, St. John's College had already been there more than a hundred years. The first Superintendent of the then "Naval School on the Severn" was Franklin Buchanan. In a short time, a four-year curriculum with summer training cruises was initiated. The Civil War split the Academy in microcosm as it split the country. Classmates separated to face each another at another time and place as enemies. The Academy's buildings, from which the cadets had moved to Newport, Rhode Island, became hospitals for the battlefields of Virginia. Otherwise Annapolis was little disturbed by the Civil War.

With the emergence of Baltimore as the principal port of the Chesapeake, Annapolis settled into being an agricultural center and a seafood harvesting market. It is still the capital of the State of Maryland, using the oldest state house in the nation as the meeting place for its legislature. Annapolis' chief raison d'etre is the Academy, but its growing importance as a tourist-attracting hub keeps this city of 25,000 energetic.

EXPLORING ANNAPOLIS

Annapolis is primarily a walking town but to get there almost requires a car. The Washington-Baltimore International Airport is the closest commercial airport but Washington National Airport is not much farther away. Municipal parking is provided at various locations but on-street parking is very strictly limited to two hours. There is a shuttle bus service between the Navy/Marine Stadium parking lot and downtown.

The town is sprinkled with historical buildings: residential, commercial, and governmental. Many are privately owned and unavailable for viewing. All the dozen or so which can be visited were built in the mid-1700s and have seen some restoration. The **Maryland State House** is particularly proud of its historical significance both as the first peace-time capitol building of the United States and as the oldest capitol building in continuous legislative use. Within a half-dozen blocks of the State House are the exquisitly restored **Paca House** and **Gardens, Brice House, Chase-Lloyd House,** and **Hammond-Harwood House.** Five historic hostelries in the city have been restored to use as taverns and inns. These cluster around Church Circle and State Circle in the center of the town. These charming country-inns-in-town range in size from the four guest rooms, restaurant, and tavern of the **Reynolds Tavern** to the 55 guest rooms, meeting rooms, and banquet room of the **Governor Calvert House.** Also on State Circle is the old **Treasury,** the oldest legislative building in use in Maryland.

A short walk from State Circle along North Street will bring the visitor to the south corner of **St. John's College** with its lovely campus bounded by St. John's Street, College Avenue, College Creek, and King George Street. The latter, if taken in the opposite direction (i.e., south) leads at its other end to the visitors' gate of the **United States Naval Academy.** The campus is impressive but serene. It is hard, however, to resist a thrill at the sight of all those arrow-straight young leaders-to-be in their neat uniforms.

The maybe not as historical but very much enjoyable area of Annapolis is centered around **City Dock.** Here the **Market Space** is surrounded by hotels, restaurants, shops, and boats, boats, boats. Charter boats, tour boats, fishing boats, working boats, and playing boats. Ferries, dinghys, yachts, canoes, power launches, and, as the writer found delightedly one early morning, even a 52-foot schooner moored beside the balcony of a second floor room in the Hilton Inn above City Dock.

PRACTICAL INFORMATION FOR ANNAPOLIS

PLACES TO STAY

HOTELS, MOTELS, AND INNS. Annapolis is small and rooms are sometimes scarce, especially during the summer season, when the Boat Show is in town, or when the Naval Academy is graduating a new class of Midshipmen. Book early and hope for the best, but don't be surprised if your motel is a very long hike from the water.

Hilton Inn. *Expensive to Deluxe.* On the harbor, with boats, boats, and boats below your window and the Academy only a monkey's-fist throw away. 80 Compromise, at St. Mary's St., 21401; 268–7555 or (800) 446–3811. 135 rooms in an attractive, efficient inn. Waterfront bar and penthouse restaurant. AE, CB, DC, MC, V.

Maryland Inn. *Expensive.* 16 Church Circle, at Main, 21401; 263–2641. Built in the late 1700s and restored in 1953, this charming red-brick, three-story inn has 44 rooms. Bar and Treaty of Paris restaurant. AE, CB, DC, MC, V.

Holiday Inn. *Moderate to Expensive.* Out of the harbor area, but convenient; near US 50 and 301; 210 Holiday Inn Ct., Rt. 301 and 450, 21401; 224–3150. A full-line, attractive motel, with 221 rooms. Major credit cards.

Econo Lodge. *Inexpensive.* 591 Revell Hwy. (US 50 and 301) 21401; 974–4440 or (800) 446–6900. 74 rooms. AE, MC, V.

Thr-Rift Inn. *Inexpensive.* 2542 Riva Rd., 21401; 224–2800 or (800) 636–5169. 150 rooms, three miles west on US 50. Restaurant nearby. AE, MC, V.

Robert Johnson House. *Expensive.* 22 State Circle, 21401; 263–2641. 30 rooms in a four-story hotel. Rates less off-season. Continental breakfasts. AE, MC, V.

Academy Hotel. *Moderate.* 200 Revell Hwy., 21401; 757–2222. 56 units, with restaurant nearby. AE, CB, DC, MC, V.

Annapolis Terrace Hotel. *Moderate.* 71 Revell Hwy., 21401; 757–3030. 51 units, with outdoor pool and restaurant. AE, CB, DC, MC, V.

Climat de France. *Moderate to Expensive.* 2451 Riva Rd., 21401; 224–4317 or (800) 4-FRANCE. A 59-room hotel, with restaurant. AE, CB, DC, MC, V.

Howard Johnson. *Moderate.* 170 Revell Hwy., 21401; 757–1600. 100-unit motel, with a 24-hour restaurant and pool. AE, DC, MC, V.

Gibson's Lodgings. *Moderate to Expensive.* 110 and 114 Prince George St., 21401; 268–5555. An interesting 14-room inn, with off-street parking and restaurant nearby. Continental breakfast.

Governor Calvert House. *Moderate to Expensive.* State Circle, 21401; 263–2206. Like Maryland Inn, above, an Historic Inn of Annapolis. 46 rooms, 9 restored Victorian. Restaurant nearby. Underground parking. AE, CB, DC, MC, V.

PLACES TO EAT

RESTAURANTS. Annapolis has no shortage of excellent restaurants. Not too surprising, Bay fish and crab are featured fare, but if seafood isn't your thing, there's a restaurant for every taste. The following is a selection only; there isn't space to list them all. We've given special mention to a few that the editors feel are especially noteworthy, either for the food, the view, of the restaurant's decor; you're certain to find some favorites of your own.

Treaty of Paris Restaurant. *Moderate to Expensive.* (See Maryland Inn); 263–2641. Breakfast, lunch, and dinner, with a continental menu. Reservations a must. Restaurant and King of France Tavern worthy of note. AE, MC, V.

Chart House. *Moderate to Expensive.* Part of the chain, but the chain's formula is good—good food in generous portions on the water, with boats in their slips and a harbor view just beyond your table. Chart House restaurants feature a comfortable lounge, where you can sip your predinner cocktail while waiting for your table in the restaurant's sprawling, busy dining room. Seafood, of course. Reservations not a must, but a good idea. Major credit cards.

Hilton Inn's (Penthouse Restaurant). *Moderate to Expensive.* Hilton Inn, on the harbor, above the Town Docks' 268–7555. Whatever they're calling it this season, the Hilton's top-floor restaurant's window tables have some of the best harbor views in town. Maryland crab featured, but the menu is fairly international. Major credit cards.

Harbour House. *Moderate to Expensive.* 87 Prince George St., just off City Dock; 268–0771. Open from shortly before noon until almost midnight. Harbor House is in an old dock warehouse. Fish, and on-site baking. AE, MC, V.

Middletown Tavern. *Moderate to Expensive.* 2 Market Pl., overlooking the harbor; 263–3323. Stuffed sole and black bean soup, with a salad bar. Open till 1 A.M., with a bar that's open till 2. Outdoor dining at a restored 1750 building. MC, V.

Slightly Out of Town

Chesapeake Inn. *Moderate to Expensive.* Two miles west of the Bay Bridge on US 50 and 301, 321 Revell Hwy., 21401; 757–1717. A Chesapeake standby, Busch's Chesapeake Inn features on-site baking and crab imperial. Bar. Open from 11 till 11, later on Saturday. Rustic, nautical decor. AE, DC, MC, V.

Hemingway's. *Moderate to Expensive.* (See Eastern Shore) Hemingway's bayfront restaurant and crab house is near the eastern end of the Bay Bridge, Stevensville. Outdoor dining with a super view of the Bay. Soft shell crab—of course! 643–2722. AE, MC, V.

Foxchase Tavern. *Moderate to Expensive.* 2973 Solomons Islands Rd., Edgewater, 21037, on Rt. 2, just south of town over new South River Bridge; 956–5858. The tavern specializes in *beef*—prime ribs or steaks—but there's also seafood, of course. Lunch and dinner and a special Sunday brunch. An attractive hunt-club decor. AE, MC, V.

Fred's. *Moderate to Expensive.* 2973 Solomons Island Rd., at Parole, 21401; 224–2386. Italian-American, from veal parmigiana to crab cakes in a Victorian setting. Closed Thanksgiving, but usually open from 11 to 10 P.M. AE, DC, MC, V.

The Galleon. *Expensive.* 2840 Solomon Islands Rd., Edgewater, 21037; two miles south on Rt. 2; 266–8011. Seafood and steak, with baking on premises. Pianist and galleon decor. Open from 11 till 10, later on weekends. Sunday brunch. Closed Christmas. AE, CB, DC, MC, V.

Whitehall Inn. *Moderate.* Seven miles east of town on US 50 and 301, a mile and a half west of the Bay Bridge; Revell Hwy., 21401; 757–3737. 11 till 10, Sunday at noon. Flounder and crab, plus chicken, in an attractive rustic decor. AE, DC, MC, V.

THINGS TO SEE AND DO

THE HARBOR. It all starts at the harbor, and the harbor is why it's all there. Annapolis is a nautical town, loaded to the gunnels with docks, marinas, seafood restaurants, yacht chandleries, and the U.S. Naval Academy. Home port or a mecca for Bay sailors, Annapolis is also a major stopover haven for yachtsmen cruising north or south along the New England to Florida waterway. If you don't like boats, you may not like Annapolis. But if you do, this charming Chesapeake port could be the next best thing to paradise.

BOATING. Harbor cruise, Severn River and Spa Creek tours, day cruise to St. Michaels on the Eastern shore. Chesapeake Marine Tours, P.O. Box 3350, Annapolis, MD 21403, 268–7600.

SAILING CHARTERS. Charters available with or without a captain. Chesapeake and Coastal Charters, P.O. Box 3322, Annapolis, MD 21403, (800) 638–SAIL or (301) 268–0068. Sailing yachts and trawlers, captained; 27-foot to 52-foot, hour, day, or weekend; Annapolis Bay Charter, Inc., 7074 Bembe Beach Road, Annapolis, MD 21403.

SEASONAL EVENTS. World's Largest Sailboat Show, 1st week in October; boats on display in the water; fee.

TOURS. U.S. Naval Academy. Tourist information at Visitors' Gate #1 Rickett's Hall; guided tour recommended. (There are dull academic places that have no interest for a visitor.) Tours are perhaps somewhat long for senior citizens and the handicapped. Arrangements for bus transport between major stops can be made (one week advance). Among points of interest are the crypt of John Paul Jones, Bancroft Hall (world's largest dormitory), and the Naval Museum. Naval Academy Tour Guide Service Annapolis, MD 21402, 263–6933.

HISTORIC ANNAPOLIS. Several agencies conduct walking tours of old houses, inns, and governmental buildings: Historic Annapolis Tours, Inc., 267–8149; Three Centuries Tour, 263–5401; Town Crier (pedicab, summer only), 263–7330.

Waterfront. City Dock is the center of the Annapolis waterfront. Strolling areas, easy distances between restaurants, hotels, marinas, specialty shops, galleries, the Market House, and such scheduled attractions as the Maryland Clam Festival every August.

TOURIST INFORMATION. For more information on any of Annapolis' attractions contact: Greater Annapolis Chamber of Commerce, Annapolis, MD 21401; (301) 268–7676, or Maryland Department of Economic Development, Tourist Division, 45 Calvert Street, Annapolis, MD 21401; (301) 269–3517.

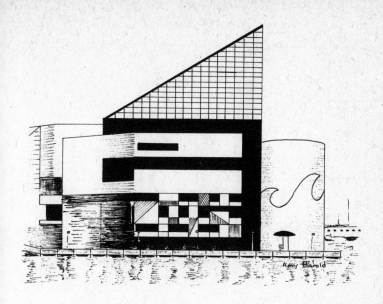

BALTIMORE

by
JAMES DAY

There was a time when if a Baltimorean went away from home and told
people where he came from, they would point at him and hoot that,
yes, they knew Baltimore. Wasn't it that dirty little town on the way
to Washington, full of smokestacks and gritty streets?

But the truth was then, and even more so now, that Baltimore,
perched near the top of the Bay, has always been one of the more livable
towns in the United States. The difference now is that it's a little more
livable and that its "renaissance" of the last 15 years has opened its
secret to the rest of the world. Baltimore is small enough to be managa-
ble and small enough so visitors can walk or easily ride from the harbor
area to most of its attractions. It has, so far at least, managed to reap
the benefits of a business and tourist boom—envied by many other

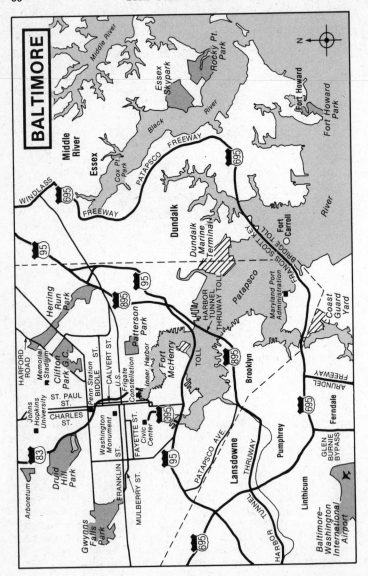

BALTIMORE

N

cities—while retaining much of its indigenous charm. These include its ethnic and blue-collar neighborhoods of proudly maintained marble steps; its food, based of course on the Bay and the state's rich farmland —oysters, clams, crabs, tomatoes, fruit, corn; its Southern hospitality; and its own peculiar dialect, where oil is "awl," iron is "arn," and below is "blow."

But Baltimore is also large enough to have, again within easy reach of the harbor, some of the best art museums in the world, a wealth of historical homes and sites, entirely restored neighborhoods of town houses, a healthy availability of hotel rooms, and a boom of first-rate restaurants encompassing everything from fancy French to local sea-food specialties.

At the heart of all this is the harbor, the reason for Baltimore's being when the colony of Maryland was granted to George Calvert, Lord Baltimore, in 1632. The three areas most closely identified with Baltimore's place on the Bay (actually it lies on the Patapsco River) are:

Federal Hill. Just south of the Inner Harbor, this steep hill with its fine view of the city and the head of the river was for years a lookout for shipowners awaiting the arrival of their vessels. Shipyards surrounded the hill on the water side. During the Civil War, Union guns were mounted on the hill and aimed at the city to keep the strategic town in the Union's ranks. The area is now a busy neighborhood of renovated homes, parks, and markets.

Fell's Point. First owned by English ship builder William Fell in the early 1700s, this harbor area lies east of the city center and retains much of its hard-working, warehouse-filled atmosphere. But it also has many renovated homes, new eateries, and nightspots.

The Inner Harbor. The pride of the city fathers, this is the showcase of Baltimore's rebirth. It is the home of Harborplace (the nationally renowned waterfront shopping and restaurant center developed by James Rouse), the National Aquarium, the U.S. Frigate *Constellation*, open-air concerts, and docking facilities. It is also often the visitor's central point of reference. This area is within easy walking distance of Federal Hill. Slightly farther along is Fell's Point. And to the north stretches the city's center, boasting its new office buildings and hotels, long stretches of shops and restaurants and, about 10 blocks directly north, the beautiful and historic Mount Vernon, a place of parks, museums, and attractive renovated town houses.

PRACTICAL INFORMATION FOR BALTIMORE

PLACES TO STAY

HOTELS, INNS, AND B&B'S. Once there were only a
few, slightly decrepit hotels in the downtown area, but
in the wake of Baltimore's business and tourist boom
new hotels have sprouted up at a fast rate, mostly in the

Inner Harbor. Many have special, less expensive weekend or vacation rates; call
for details. The following selection also includes some bed-and-breakfast establishments and inns, which usually provide continental breakfast, antique-filled
rooms, and other homelike amenities. B&B's are being added all the time. Call
B&B Reservations Service (33 West St., Annapolis, MD 21401, (301) (269–
6232) for the lastest information and reservations.

The following categories pertain to double occupancy at regular rates:
Deluxe, $100 and up; *Expensive,* $75 to $100; *Moderate,* $40 to $75; and *Inex-
pensive,* $40 and under.

The Brookshire Hotel. *Expensive to Deluxe.* 120 E. Lombard St.; 625–1300.
Close to the Inner Harbor and includes luxury suites. Two restaurants.

Hyatt Regency. *Expensive to Deluxe.* 300 Light St.; 528–1234. An all-glass
front that overlooks the Inner Harbor. Three restaurants and an indoor pool.
Easy access to the Convention Center.

Omni International. *Expensive to Deluxe.* 101 W. Fayette St.; 752–1100.
Shops, restaurant, and piano bar. In the heart of downtown.

Peabody Court. *Expensive to Deluxe.* 612 Cathedral St.; 727–7101. A Euro-
pean-style luxury hotel with a brasserie, top-floor gourmet restaurant, marbled
baths, and international telex services.

Admiral Fell Inn. *Moderate to Expensive.* 328 S. Broadway; 522–7377. A
B&B in Fell's Point with all the amenities and a van to take you to the city center
and Inner Harbor.

Baltimore Plaza. *Moderate to Expensive.* 11 S. Eutaw St.; 962–0202. Includes
a waterfall in the lobby, lounge and restaurant, and babysitters on call.

Belvedere Hotel. *Moderate to Expensive.* 1 E. Chase St.; 332–1000. Overlooking Mount Vernon and most of the rest of the city. Top-floor bar, restaurant,
and shops.

Shirley House. *Moderate to Expensive.* 205 W. Madison St.; 728–6550. A
restored house in Mount Vernon with attention to antiques and detail; continental breakfast and evening aperitifs.

Society Hill Hotel. *Moderate to Expensive.* 58 W. Biddle St.; 837–3630. A
combination hotel, B&B, and inn; with continental breakfast and antiques.
Restaurant.

Tremont Hotel. *Moderate to Expensive.* 8 E. Pleasant St.; 576–1200. Restaurant, lounge, admission to athletic club, all luxury appointments.

Comfort Inn. *Inexpensive to Moderate.* 24 W. Franklin St.; 576–8400. Near Mount Vernon, with bar and restaurant; across from Baltimore's famous Enoch Pratt Free Library.

Days Inn. *Inexpensive.* 100 Hopkins Plaza; 576–1000. Outdoor pool and restaurant.

Holiday Inn-Downtown. *Moderate to Expensive.* Howard and Lombard Sts.; 685–3500. One of the first new hotels in Baltimore; rooftop restaurant and lounge.

Tremont Plaza. *Moderate to Expensive.* 222 St. Paul Place; 727–2222. Restaurant and pool, with a wide variety of room sizes and plans.

Hostels. The Baltimore International Youth Hostel, 12 W. Mulberry St. (576–8880), has bunk room beds for $7–$11, depending on the time of year and membership status.

PLACES TO EAT

RESTAURANTS AND RAW BARS. Since the first settler gazed upon a plump oyster, Baltimoreans have had a wonderful time eating. A Baltimorean is perhaps happiest when the Orioles are winning, tomatoes are in season, and the table is covered with spicy steamed crabs and pitchers of cold beer.

A good starting place to join the native in epicurean bliss is a raw bar, found at the city's large markets, Harborplace, and many bars. Clams and oysters on the half shell, steamed shrimp, and mussels are slurped and gobbled amid a pleasant din of chatter and a cross-section of the city's populace. Crab houses, listed below, provide the pleasure of the area's renowned steamed crabs.

But Baltimore eating is not just seafood. The downtown area is increasingly dotted with first-rate steak houses, continental restaurants, and ethnic eateries. A stroll around the harbor area—Fell's Point, Little Italy, Federal Hill, or Harborplace—will reveal many worthy restaurants. Mount Vernon's restaurant row has something for every taste and pocketbook. Remember, our listing is merely a selection; Fodor's editors would appreciate hearing of your personal discoveries.

The cost of an a la carte dinner is the basis of our price range: *Expensive,* $22 and above; *Moderate,* $15–$22; *Inexpensive,* under $15.

The Brass Elephant. *Expensive.* 924 N. Charles St., 547–8480. Northern Italian fare in an elegant setting. Homemade, tasty desserts.

Chart House. *Expensive.* 601 E. Pratt St., 539–6616. Perhaps the best view of the harbor from an eatery. Wide ranging menu with a raw bar.

The Conservatory. *Expensive.* In the Peabody Court hotel, 612 Cathedral St., 727–7101. Just plain elegant, with a French gourmet menu and a rooftop view of Mount Vernon.

Danny's. *Expensive.* 1201 N. Charles St., 539–1393. One of Baltimore's most famous, with a wide range of seafood and meat dishes. If you see a sign on the outside saying "Whales," don't worry. It's just announcing the presence of soft-shelled crabs, a Maryland treat if there ever was one.

John Eagar Howard Room. *Expensive.* Charles and Chase streets, in the Belvedere Hotel, 547–8220. Fancy, old-fashioned setting, with veal and beef specialties as well as lighter continental fare. A trip back to the opulence of turn-of-the-century Baltimore.

The Orchid. *Expensive.* 419 N. Charles St., 837–0081. An intriguing and popular combination of French and Oriental dishes.

The Prime Rib. *Expensive.* 1101 N. Calvert St., 539–1804. A taste of New York in the Mount Vernon area, with a piano bar, lush setting, juicy beef, and seafood. Where the natives go to really treat themselves.

Tio Pepe's. *Expensive.* 10 E. Franklin St., 539–4675. The boneless duck, the shrimp with garlic, and the whole array of Spanish dishes make this a very popular spot, which in turn means it can be hard to get the reservations you want.

Bertha's. *Moderate.* 734 S. Broadway, 327–5795. Famous for its mussels, done up in several ways, its soups and its paella, Bertha's has long been a Fell's Point landmark and watering hole.

Haussner's. *Moderate.* 3244 Eastern Ave., 327–8365. A Baltimore landmark because of its art-covered walls and relatively simple, solid and tasty American and German food.

Little Italy, a few blocks east of the Inner Harbor. Even if it weren't for the restaurants, this area of rowhouses and thick dialect is a fine place for a stroll. If the walking has made you hungry, there's plenty to choose from, including: **Chiapparelli's,** 237 High St., 837–0309; **Sabatino's,** 901 Fawn St., 727–9414; and **Velleggia's,** 204 High St., 685–2620. All are known for their salads and veal, and have extensive menus. And each is a gathering place for local politicians and other well-knowns. Moderate prices at all three.

Maison Marconi. *Moderate.* 106 W. Saratoga St., 752–9286. A long-time favorite among locals for genteel dining. They pour your drinks at the table and change the menu frequently to incorporate the lastest fresh catch or harvest.

Martick's. *Moderate.* 214 W. Mulberry St., 752–5155. A former speakeasy and longtime hangout for artists, this tin-plated room is the setting for tasty and original French food. Veal dishes, duck, and homemade pâté are popular.

Olde Obrycki's Crab House. *Moderate.* 1729 E. Pratt St., 732–6399. A local favorite for years for its steamed crabs and crab dishes. The crab cocktail is much in demand.

Zingaro's. *Moderate.* 400 E. Pratt St., 837–2620. Changing menus as well as always reliable standards, including its homemade tomato sauce and pasta, make this one of the city's most popular Italian restaurants.

2110. *Moderate.* 2110 N. Charles St., 727–6692. Fresh pâtés and a simple setting have made this one of Baltimore's more enjoyable French restaurants.

Akbar. *Inexpensive.* 823 N. Charles St., 539–0944. Indian food. From mild to outrageously hot, Akbar has something interesting for just about everyone. Its rogan josh, marinated lamb, is particularly popular.

The American Cafe. *Inexpensive.* Light Street Pavillon, Harborplace, 962–8800. Light gourmet food, soups and drinks, all with a harbor view.

Gunning's Crab House. *Inexpensive.* 3901 S. Hanover St., 354–0085. A traditional South Baltimore crab house, with globs of spicy sauce on the hard-shelled, steamed crabs.

Louie's Bookstore and Cafe. *Inexpensive.* 518 N. Charles St., 962–1224. A great place for tasty salads, pastries, and cappucino. The art on the wall is an ever-changing display by local artists.

The Museum Cafe. *Inexpensive.* 10 Art Museum Drive, in the Baltimore Museum of Art, 235–3930. With a view of the sculpture garden and a menu that is fresh and inventive. Known for its pesto.

THINGS TO SEE AND DO

BOATING. Docking and anchorage facilities are expanding in the harbor area. Free anchorage is available in Fell's Point and the Inner Harbor, as space permits, and docking fees start at 25¢ to 50¢ per boat foot. In the Inner Harbor, contact the city dockmaster (396–3174, Channel 38) or Inner Harbor Marina (837–5339). Baltimore's Anchorage Marina in Fell's Point can be reached at 522–4007 or Channel 16.

Harbor Boating, in the Inner Harbor near the *Constellation* (547–0900), rents sailboats and paddle boats from spring to fall. The Ski Shoppe (833–1101) also rents sailboats.

HOW TO GET AROUND. From the airport. Airport limo service, located on the ground floor of the Baltimore-Washington International Airport, about 10 miles from city center, provides transportation to the city's major hotels for less than $8.

By subway. Baltimore's new subway costs 75¢, 85¢ to or from Reistertown Road Plaza, and runs from downtown to the plaza, with stops in between, Mon.–Fri. 5 A.M. to 8 P.M., Sat. 8 A.M. to 8 P.M.

By bus. The Mass Transit Administration (539–5000) runs the citywide bus system. The basic fare is 75¢. Call for point-to-point instructions.

By trolley. The newest addition to Baltimore's transit system is a small fleet of replica trolley cars that travel around the Inner Harbor and up Charles Street to historic and beautiful Mount Vernon. At 25¢ the trolley routes provide an easy, pleasant, and cheap way to get around downtown. The Inner Harbor route runs Sun.–Thurs. from 11 A.M. to 10 P.M., Fri. and Sat. 11–11, and includes Little Italy, the Aquarium, and Harborplace shopping pavilions. The Charles Street trolley operates from 11 A.M. to 8:30 P.M., Monday through Saturday. Stops are marked by special "Trolley" signs. The trolleys can also be chartered for private groups. Call 396–4259.

By Water. There is daily water taxi service between major harbor points, mid-April through mid-October. The taxi is based near the *Constellation* in the Inner Harbor.

HISTORIC SITES AND HOMES. Basilica of the Assumption of the Blessed Virgin Mary. Cathedral and Mulberry Sts. (727–3564). The first Roman Catholic cathedral in the U.S. Open daily, 7–6 P.M. Tours available. Free.

Carroll Mansion and the 1840 House. Lombard and Front Sts. (396–3523). Restored last home of Charles Carroll, signer of the Declaration of Independence, with period furniture and art. Adjacent house restored to show how people lived in early Baltimore. Free.

The U.S. Frigate Constellation. Constellation Dock, Pratt St. (539–1797). Built in Baltimore in 1797, the restored "Yankee Racehorse" was the first commissioned ship in the U.S. Navy. Open daily, seasonal hours. Small admission fee.

Flag House and 1812 Museum. 844 E. Pratt St. (837–1793). Home of Mary Pickersgill, who made the flag that flew over Fort McHenry. Mon.–Sat. 10–4; Sun. 1–4. Small admission fee.

Fort McHenry. Fort Ave. off Key Highway (539–3678). Birthplace of the "Star Spangled Banner" and historic military site. Open daily. Free.

H.L. Mencken House. 1524 Hollins St. (396–7997). Wed.–Sun. 10–5. Small admission fee.

Minnie V. Pier 1, Pratt St. (685–3750). A working oyster boat, the *Minnie V* visits Baltimore for educational programs and harbor tours. Hours vary. Free.

Mount Clare Mansion. Monroe St. and Washington Blvd. (837–3262). Built in 1754, this is the restored home of Barrister Charles Carroll. Tues.–Sat., 11–4; Sun. 1–4. Small admission charge.

Peabody Institute. 1 E. Mount Vernon Pl. (659–8100). The nation's oldest music school with a beautiful library where Dos Passos once worked. Library is open weekdays, 9–5. Free Tuesday concerts during the school year.

Poe House. 203 N. Amity St. (396–7932). Contains the cold, tiny garret where Edgar Allan Poe wove his dark tales from 1832–35. Hours vary. Small admission fee. Poe is buried nearby at the Westminster Burying Ground.

Shot Tower. 801 E. Fayette St. (396–5894). This 234-foot brick tower was used in the 1800s to make shot by pouring lead from the top into a vat of cold water at the bottom. Daily 10–4. Free.

Washington Monument. 700 N. Charles St. (396–3523). In the heart of Mount Vernon, this is the first architectural monument to George Washington. Hours vary. Small admission fee.

LIVELY ARTS. The crown jewel of the music scene is the **Baltimore Symphony Orchestra**, whose home base is the Meyerhoff Symphony Hall, 1212 Cathedral St. (837–5691). The Meyerhoff also regularly has special programs. Other choices include the Baltimore Choral Arts Society (523–7070), the Baltimore Opera Company (685–0693), Johns Hopkins University's concert series (338–7164), and the Peabody Conservatory of Music (659–8124).

A healthy mix of stage performances, including classical works, experimental pieces and pre-Broadway tryouts, are available at: the **Lyric Opera House** in Mount Vernon (685–5086); the **Morris A. Mechanic Theater** in Hopkins Plaza (625–1400); **Center Stage**, 700 N. Calvert St. (332–0033); the **Theater Project**, 45 W. Preston St. (539–3091); and the Arena Players, 801 McCulloh St. (728–6500).

MARKETS. Baltimore prides itself on its large and lively public markets. They are gathering places for the natives and offer seafood, meat—fancy veal to hamhocks—and local vegetables. **Lexington Market**, Lexington and Paca Sts., is the oldest; it's been there since 1782. Others include the **Broadway Market** at Broadway and Aliceanna Sts. in Fells Point; **Hollins Market**, in H.L. Mencken's neighborhood, Carrolton St.; and the **Cross Street Market** in Federal Hill. Lazing at a market's raw bar is perhaps the best way to get to see Baltimoreans in their most natural state.

MUSEUMS. Babe Ruth Birthplace/Maryland Baseball Hall of Fame. 216 Emory St. (727–1539) includes documentaries and exhibits on the Babe and Baltimore's Orioles. Daily. Hours vary. Small admission fee.

Baltimore Art Museum. N. Charles and 33rd Sts. (396–7100). Rodin's "Thinker," largest Matisse collection in U.S., sculpture garden with cafe, and American and African art. Tues.–Fri., 10–4; Sat. and Sun. 11–6. Small fee. Thursdays free.

Baltimore Maritime Museum. Pier 4, Pratt St. (396–3854). Includes the USS *Torsk*, a World War II submarine that sank the last four Japanese ships at the end of the war, and the Lightship *Chesapeake*. Daily. Hours vary. Small admission charge.

Maryland Science Center. 601 Light St. (685–5225). Hands-on exhibits, films and planetarium. Hours vary. Small admission fee.

Museum and Library of Maryland History. 201 W. Monument St. (685–3750). Collections of furniture, prints, maps, the original manuscript of "The Star Spangled Banner," early Maryland artifacts. Tues.–Fri. 11–4:30. Sat. 9–4:30. Small admission fee.

Museum of Industry. 1415 Key Highway (727–4808). Re-creations of early industrial jobs and machines. Sat. 10–5; Sun. noon–5. Small admission fee.

The Peale Musuem. 225 Holliday St. (396–3523). This, the first Baltimore City Hall, includes exhibits of early Baltimore life. Tues.–Sun., 10–4. Free.

Pride of Baltimore. Docked in Inner Harbor. Replica of the famous Baltimore Clippers, the *Pride* travels the world as the city's floating ambassador.

Walters Art Gallery. 600 N. Charles St. (547–9000). One of the country's most famous, its exhibits span 6,000 years. Stained glass, Mesopotamian and Egyptian art, manuscripts, sculpture. Tues.–Sun., 11–5. Small admission fee. Wednesdays free.

World Trade Center. (837–4515) Next to Harborplace, the Center offers a marvelous view from its 27th-floor observatory as well as exhibits of the city's history. Open daily. $1 adults, 75¢ for children.

 SHOPPING. The most interesting shopping plan in Baltimore is to browse by area. Charles St., from Lombard to Eager Sts., is lined with art and craft galleries that include works by nationally known and local artists.

Harborplace. With its two pavillons, Harborplace houses more than 100 gourmet food stalls, crafts shops, and well-known clothing stores. Open Mon.– Sat. 10–9:30, Sun. noon to 8.

Fells Point. Fells Point is crowded with intriguing antique and maritime stores. Antique Row, on Howard St. in Mount Vernon, has more than 35 shops ranging from the posh to knickknack collections.

 SPECTATOR SPORTS. The Orioles play baseball at Memorial Stadium; the Skipjacks play hockey and the Blast play indoor soccer at the Civic Center. The Stars play USFL football in College Park.

Pimlico Race Track opens its gates at 1 P.M. during its spring and summer seasons. The Preakness, middle leg of the Triple Crown, is run at Pimlico on the third Saturday in May.

Baltimore is the mecca of lacrosse, and local colleges, including Johns Hopkins (338–8197) and Loyola College (323–1010), have home games in the spring.

For more information: Orioles, 338–1300; Skipjacks, 727–0703; Blast, 528–0100; Pimlico, 542–9400.

 TOURS AND CRUISES. Baltimore offers many tours, several by water, of the harbor and the Chesapeake shore, as well as tours of downtown Baltimore and outlying areas. Walking tours have become popular and besides being fun are easily managed in a city of Baltimore's compact size. Walking tour information is available at many hotels, the Women's Civic League (837–5425), and at the city's Office of Tourism, 752–8632.

Other tours and cruises include: About Town Tours Unlimited (592–7770) offers personalized tours of Baltimore and other areas. American Cruise Lines (800–243–6755), with 7-day bay cruises. Baltimore Rent-a-Tour (653–2998) sightseeing, walking and insomniac tours. Clipper City, tall ship touring (539–6063). Defender and Guardian (752–1515), between the harbor, Fells Pt. and Fort McHenry. Harbor Cruises (727–3113) offers lunch, dinner, and charter packages. Maryland Tours (685–4288) offers daily harbor tours. Minnie V Skipjack (522–4212) has harbor and charter tours. Minnie Tours (256–4384) includes theme tours. Tours of Mount Vernon are available by calling 592–5262. Total Picture Tours (325–1978) offers helicopter, water, and bus-limousine tours throughout the area. Tour Tapes of Baltimore (752–8632) provides three car tapes ($9.95 each, $25 for three) that direct you to and explain major sights in the city.

NIGHT LIFE. Once boringly sedate, the town is now starting to jump, with bars and clubs offering jazz, rock, new wave, and Irish music. Besides those spots listed below, there are many night entertainments to be found just by strolling in the Inner Harbor, Federal Hill, and Fell's Point areas.

Ethel's Place (1225 Cathedral St., 727–7077). Opened by local jazz singer Ethel Ennis, this club has a regular schedule of top-name jazz stars.

The Cafe Park Plaza (810 N. Charles St., 727–7772) also offers up some fine jazz shows.

8x10 (10 E. Cross St., 837–8559) provides some of the best in local and national blues and rock. Other clubs include **The Cat's Eye** (1730 Thames St., 732–9477), Irish music; the **Thirteenth Floor** in the Belvedere Hotel (Charles and Chase Sts., 539–7110), piano bar and great view.

ZOOS. Baltimore Zoo (Druid Hill Park, Druid Hill Lake Drive, 396–7102). More than a thousand animals inhabit this 150-acre zoo, including lions, giraffes, and baby animals for petting. Open daily, 10–4:20, 11–5:20 on summer Sundays. Small admission fee.

THE NATIONAL AQUARIUM. Located at Pier 3, Inner Harbor (576–3810), the Aquarium boasts more than 5,000 creatures, a rain forest, ocean tank of sharks, and a coral reef. Summer and winter hours. $5.75 adults; $4.25 students and seniors; $3 ages 3–11; under 3 free.

Amy Harold

THE UPPER BAY

It is difficult to understand why the Upper Bay is often ignored in tours of the Chesapeake region. True, it lacks the bustle and relative sophistication of Baltimore or the sunstruck pleasures of the Atlantic resorts. But the Upper Bay, where the mighty Susquehanna empties and the wild goose flies, is one of the most lush, bountiful, and historic parts of the Bay area.

The pace here is easy. The eastern shore of the Upper Bay, easily reached but still furthest away from major highways and cities, is perfect for a relaxed drive through its farmland and towns, or a cruise up its many creeks and rivers. It is a trip to a quieter time with simpler pleasures. The land and water provide a cornucopia of corn, tomatoes, fish, clams, and other seafood, all available at homegrown prices. Some, of course, are there for the catching. The area lies within the Atlantic Flyway and is renowned for its hunting opportunities. In the spring the region is crazy with dogwood and forsythia, and in the fall it becomes, except for the honking of geese, quiet and crisp, a Thanksgiving tab-

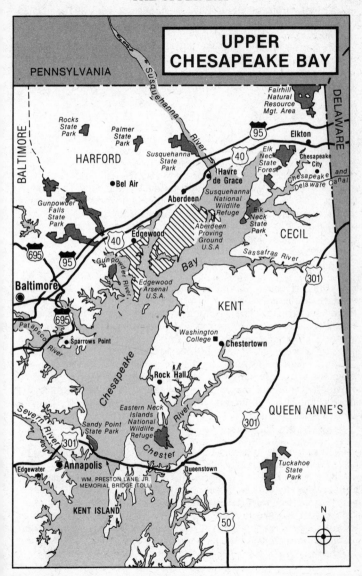

UPPER CHESAPEAKE BAY

leau. To all of this the Upper Bay's western shore adds its Bay-related commercial towns, the Susquehanna, and a history that dates back to the founding of the colonies.

Both shores boast numerous marinas and are close by Baltimore, Washington, and Interstate 95.

The clearest introduction to the Upper Bay is by county, which is also how the natives often identify themselves.

Baltimore County

The county, only part of which is directly connected to the water, surrounds Baltimore City in a crablike grip. It was founded in 1659. Its Bay side, the lower eastern side of the country, is ribboned with inlets, rivers, creeks, marinas, and Bay-related industries. Once-mighty Sparrows Point, site of steel producing and shipbuilding, juts into the Bay. Farther north and inland, the county provides Baltimore with some of its busiest and most populous suburbs. As the county stretches north to the Pennsylvania line, it becomes a place of rolling fields, genteel mansions, and cross-country horse racing.

Harford County

To the northeast of Baltimore County, Harford begins, especially in its more northern reaches, to show the country air of the Upper Bay. It changes from marsh to piedmont as one travels north and has long been known for its love of horses and country-style horse racing. It is home of the U.S. Army's Aberdeen Proving Ground, complete with a museum of weapons, and the historic towns of Bel Air and Havre de Grace. Its state parks offer an uncluttered view of the land as it was when the first settlers arrived, and the county has made an effort to provide exhibits and museums of how people lived and worked. Its shore is known for its marinas and its easy access to deeper water.

Cecil County

Cecil sits on the uppermost reaches of the Bay and is bordered by both Pennsylvania and Delaware. It is, in effect, the first or most northern of the Eastern Shore counties. Bordered by the Susquehanna and traversed by the Chesapeake and Delaware Canal and I-95, much of its commercial life is linked with the north. Captain John Smith first visited what is now the county in 1608. Elkton, the county seat, was for years a nortorious place for out-of-staters to come to be married in haste. But the county's place in history goes back much further. Lying along a main north-south route of travel Cecil County saw a busy time and many troops in the Revolutionary War. Restored taverns and homes now mark the routes. The county soon became one of the young nation's busiest grain and paper producers. Chesapeake City is a quiet and charming town that is increasingly popular with sightseers.

Kent County

The oldest county on the Eastern Shore, Kent County lies south of Cecil and is the epitome—in terms of gently rolling land, restored buildings, and a myriad of inlets to the Bay—of the Upper Bay. Chestertown, a bustling port in the 18th Century, is now the beautifully preserved and restored home of Washington College. The Sassafras River in the north is one of the most enchanting streams in the Bay country.

PRACTICAL INFORMATION
FOR THE UPPER BAY

PLACES TO STAY

HOTELS AND MOTELS. Though slightly higher in cost than its country cousins, Baltimore City's hotels provide the most accessible and most plentiful accommodations in the lower western section of the Upper Bay. (See the Baltimore section of this guide.) Accommodations in the rest of the Upper Bay range from small roadside motels to charming restored historic hotels in some of the towns. Off-season rates, weekend rates, and special package deals are sometimes available, and the general rates are clearly less than city-center prices. Bed and breakfast establishments, more common in Kent than in the other counties, are included in this list, and up-to-date information on the ever-expanding B&B industry can be had by contacting The Maryland Registry, 33 West St., Annapolis, MD 21401 (269–6232) or Amanada's Bed and Breakfast, Ltd., P.O. Box 42, Long Green MD 21092 (665–1333).

Many of the towns are so small and what they offer so obvious that the addresses are simply a route number. Don't be discouraged. The route inside a town is often only a block or so long and the establishment is easily found. The following rates are based on double-occupancy during the usual tourist season: *Expensive,* $70 and up; *Moderate,* $40–$70; *Inexpensive,* $40 and under.

Harford County

Best Western Red Coach Motor Inn. *Moderate.* 763 Bel Air Ave., Aberdeen (272–8500). Pool, near Aberdeen Proving Ground and weapons museum.

Econo Lodge. There are two Econo Lodges *(Inexpensive)* in the Aberdeen area, each with a restaurant and lounge: Rt. 22 and I-95 (272–5500); and close by on Rt. 22 (679–3133).

Holiday Inn. There are also two Holiday Inns in the area, both in the *Moderate* range: 793 W. Belair Rd. (272–6000); and the Holiday Inn **Chesapeake House,** 1007 Beards Hill Rd. (272–8100).

Sheraton Aberdeen. *Moderate.* 980 Beards Hill Rd. (273–6300). Restaurant, pool, nightclub, and game room.

Cecil County

County officials are refreshingly honest about the lack—for now—of first-rate lodging in the county. There are plans to rectify this, and updates can be obtained by calling the county's Tourism Coordinator (398–0200, ext. 144). Lodging can be found in Chestertown, of course, or down the road in Harford County.

Kent County

Drayton Manor. *Inexpensive.* Coopers Lane, Worton (778–2869). Outdoor pool, tennis court, restaurant, and bowling alley.

Foxley Manor Motel. *Moderate.* Rt. 213, Chestertown (778–3200).

Great Oak Landing Resort and Conference Center. Chestertown (778–2100). *Moderate.* Includes breakfast and dinner. Tennis, restaurant, marina, beach, and golf course available.

The Imperial Hotel. *Expensive.* High near Queen St., Chestertown (778–5000). Victorian decor, rather lavish appointments.

Inn at Mitchell House. *Expensive.* Rt. 21 south of Chestertown (778–5000). Antiques, B&B format with full breakfast, on a 10-acre site.

Kitty Knight House. *Moderate.* Rt. 213, Georgetown (648–5305). Live entertainment, restaurant, boating nearby.

Rolph's Wharf Inn. *Expensive.* Wharf Road, Chestertown (778–1988). Bed and breakfast style with homemade cakes and live entertainment at night. Restaurant, lounge, pool, marina.

White Swan Tavern. 231 High St., Chestertown (778–2300). B&B with restaurant nearby and museum.

Ye Lantern Inn. *Inexpensive.* Ericsson Avenue, Betterton (348–5809). Beach nearby.

PLACES TO EAT

RESTAURANTS. There is no place better to get the best in Chesapeake Bay than around the Upper Bay. The land provides sweet corn and other vegetables, while the water provides clams, oysters, numerous varieties of fish, and crabs. The food is simply prepared, but the tastes are exquisite and usually moderately priced. Waterfront dining along the rivers and canals is especially enjoyable.

The cost of an à la carte dinner is the basis of our price range: *Expensive,* $25 and up; *Moderate,* $14–$25; *Inexpensive,* under $14.

Harford County

Bay Steamer. *Inexpensive.* Foot of Franklin St. in Havre de Grace, on the Susquehanna River (939–3626). As the name implies, good, simple native fare stressing fresh seafood.

Cagney's. *Moderate.* 2607 Bel Air Rd., Fallston (877–1610). Seafood and simple fare in a pleasant, easy setting.

Colonel's Choice. *Inexpensive.* US 40 and Carol Ave., Aberdeen (272–6500). Italian and lobster dishes. A spot frequented by the locals.

Georgetown North. *Moderate.* 12 S. Main Street, Bel Air (879–0007). Daily seafood specials in the heart of town.

Cecil County

Archway Inn. *Inexpensive.* 2835 Crystal Beach Rd., Earleville (275–8609). Italian and seafood offerings.

Bayard House. *Moderate.* 11 Bohemia Ave., Chesapeake City (885–5040). Waterfront dining on the C&D Canal.

Conowingo Inn. *Moderate.* 373 Conwingo Rd., Rt. 1, Conowingo (378–4692). Crab specialties and Sunday buffet.

Dockside Yacht Club. *Moderate.* 605 Second St., Chesapeake City (885–5016). Waterfront dining April through October.

Fair Hill Inn. *Moderate to Expensive.* 3370 Singerly Rd., Fair Hill (398–4187). Historic country inn.

Island Inn. *Moderate.* 648 Broad St., Perryville (642–3448). Seafood.

North East Harbor House. *Moderate.* 200 Cherry St., North East (287–6800). Waterfront dining, docking available.

Schaefer's Canal House. *Moderate.* Bank Street, Chesapeake City (885–2200). Canalside dining.

Kent County

Danny's Northside. *Inexpensive.* High near Mill St., Chestertown (778–4900). Beef ribs, steamed shrimp, all-you-can-eat specials.

Fin, Fur, Feather Inn. *Moderate.* 424 Bayside, Rock Hall (639–7454). As the name implies, a little of everything. Crab cakes and chowder from the catch of the day are the house's pride.

Imperial Hotel Dining Room. *Moderate.* 208 High St., Chestertown (778–5000). French specialties in a Victorian setting.

Old Wharf Inn. *Moderate.* Foot of Cabin St., Chestertown (778–3566). Catch of the day specialties.

King and Crown. *Inexpensive.* 314 Park Row, Chestertown (778–0088). American fare, lamb chops, filets, and the ever-present crab dishes.

Rock Hall Inn. *Moderate.* Main St., Rock Hall (639–7141). A basic and popular seafood and steak house.

THINGS TO SEE AND DO

BOATING. The Upper Bay is a boater's paradise. With several major rivers flowing into the bay and countless streams, inlets, and creeks, boating in the area can range from a lazy, slow meander up a backwater creek to gaze at the cattails and wildlife to a full-fledged Chesapeake cruise. There are too many Bay marinas to list here, but after selecting the area you wish to visit, you can call the following numbers for more information: Baltimore County, 494–3648; Harford County, 838–6000; Cecil County, 398–0200; or Kent County, 778–0416. Most marinas in the area monitor Channel 16.

TOURING THE UPPER BAY. Baltimore-Washington International Airport, south of Baltimore, is little more than an hour and a half, at the most, from most parts of the Upper Bay. Other nearby airports include Philadelphia International, the Greater Wilmington Airport, the Cecil County Airpark near Elkton, and the Scheeler Field-Gill Airport near Chestertown.

The Upper Bay is very convenient to major highways. Interstate 95 and US 40 run along the western shore, while US 301, a major route for tobacco and farm produce, bisects the eastern portion of the Upper Bay. The two-span Bay Bridge ($1.25 each way) is easily reached from the Baltimore-Washington area.

CRUISES AND TOURS. Tours and cruises can be arranged through these groups: Tourism Council of the Upper Chesapeake, P.O. Box 99, Centreville, MD 21617 (758–2300); Minnie Tours, 9811 Fox Hill Road, Perry Hall, MD 21128 (256–4384); The Touring Machine, P.O. Box 177, Lutherville, MD 21093; or Three Centuries Tours, P.O. Box 29, 48 Maryland Ave., Annapolis, MD 21404 (263–5401). The Kent County Chamber of Commerce (118 N. Cross St., Chestertown, MD 21620, 778–0416) provides a detailed and interesting driving guide for the county and its towns.

Harford County

Concord Point Lighthouse. Lafayette Street, Havre de Grace. Built in 1829, this is the oldest continuously used lighthouse on the East Coast. Spectacular view of the Upper Bay.

Eden Mill. Off Rt. 136, Fawn Grove. This 1805 mill is surrounded by a 56-acre park with nature trails, a ski lift, and skating pond. Daylight hours. Free.

Ladew Topiary Gardens and Manor House. Rt. 145, 5 miles north of Jacksonville (557–9466). The 22-acre, world-famous garden features sculptured trees and shrubs. The mansion houses a collection of antiques, hunting memorabilia, and an extensive library. The house and gardens are on the National Register of Historic Places. Open mid-April through Oct., Tues.–Sat., 10–4, Sun. noon–5. Small admission fee.

Steppinghouse Museum. 461 Quaker Bottom Rd., Havre de Grace (939–2299). Farmhouse and shops exhibit the trades and skills of rural life in the late 1800s. Small admission fee.

Susquehanna Museum. Lock House, Erie and Conesto Sts., Havre de Grace. Exhibits are housed in the first lock of the old Susquehanna and Tidewater Canal. Hours vary. Donations accepted.

U.S. Army Ordnance Museum. Aberdeen Proving Ground, Rts. 40 and 22, Aberdeen. An extensive collection of small arms, artillery, tanks, and ammunition. Also houses captured German long-range railway gun nicknamed "Anzio Annie." Tues.–Sun. noon to 4:45. Free.

Cecil County

Chesapeake City Historical District. Once the center of canal-related commerce, the area is now being restored. Tours available. Call 885–5233.

107 House/Tory House. Market and Cecil Sts., Charlestown (287–8793). Restored colonial kitchen and tavern. Open third Sun., May through Sept. Free.

Mount Harmon Plantation. Grove Neck Road, Earleville (275–2721). This restored 18th-Century plantation sits on the banks of the Sassafras River and provides a detailed look at the elegance of plantation life, at least as the owners knew it. Includes main house, boxwood garden, tobacco house, and wharf. Hours vary. Small admission fee.

There are a number of restored houses that can be seen but not entered. A detailed "Historic Tour Guide," which includes a map of Revolutionary War marches by various armies, is available at the Cecil County office building in Elkton (398–0200).

C & D Canal Museum. Second St. and Bethel Rd., Chesapeake City (885–5621). The Old Lock pump house is a National Register site. Shows the history of the Chesapeake and Delaware Canal, which links the Upper Bay with Delaware Bay. Daily 8–4, Sun. 10–6.

Historical Society Museum. 135 East Main St. (398–0914). Exhibits include a country store and the first local schoolhouse. Mon.–Thurs., noon–4.

Upper Bay Museum. Walnut St., North East (287–5718). Includes exhibits of decoy making, duck hunting devices, guns, boats, and fishing tools—all native to the region. Summer Sundays, 9–4 and by appointment.

Kent County

Many of the historically interesting homes and sites are private but can be found in walking tours of the county's towns. The Kent County Historical Society, on Church Alley near Queen St., and the Chamber of Commerce at 118

N. Cross St. (778–0416), provide tours, open-house events, and guides for walking tours of Chestertown and other areas.

There is also a detailed and interesting driving tour of the county provided by the Chamber of Commerce.

Betterton. On the Sassafras River, Betterton was once a busy beach resort. Nearby is Still Pond, where women first voted in Maryland in 1908.

Rock Hall. A small town (1,600) with a deep harbor, Rock Hall is a fine example of many Kent County fishing communities.

The Historical Society's Geddes-Piper House. Church Alley near Queen St. (778–3499). The Society continues to develop its museum and library of early regional art and furnishings, written records, and photographs. May through Oct., Sat. and Sun., 1–4.

Rock Hall Museum. Municipal Building, South Main St., Rock Hall (778–7311). Exhibits include paintings, boat models, the country's first X-ray machines. Daily 2–4:30. Free.

Washington College. Washington and Campus Aves., Chestertown. Includes the Middle, East, and West Halls, dating from 1845 and standing on the site of the original college, which started in 1783 and where Washington received a law degree in 1789. Washington is the nation's tenth oldest college and Maryland's first.

HUNTING AND FISHING. The Upper Bay is a fisherman's paradise, a hunter's dream, and a sailor's fantasy. For more information on licensing and regulations, see the Eastern Shore section of this guide. Native and transient wildlife may be seen but not harmed at **Remington Farms,** Route 20 north of Rock Hall. Remington Farms is a 2,000-acre wildlife research area that includes nature trails for self-guide tours. Another wildlife viewing and learning center is the **Eastern Neck National Wildlife Refuge,** Route 445, south of Rock Hall. This area includes marshes, coves, and ponds, with fall and winter feeding grounds for migrating Canada geese.

SHOPPING. Antiques and water-related native crafts —decoys, hunting boats, etc.—are the most interesting and ubiquitous items for sale in the Upper Bay. Many of the restored sections of the region's small towns include at least one antique and crafts shop. Shops include: Flyway Gallery, Route 213, Cecilton, Cecil County (275–8562). Wildlife and Bay art. Gateway Gallery, 208 George St., Chesapeake City, Cecil County (885–2270). Local and original art works. Gallery 5, Cannon and Cross streets, Chestertown, Kent County (778–1966). Original arts and crafts.

LIVELY ARTS. Local production companies include the **Covered Bridge Theater,** 105 Railroad Ave., Elkton, Cecil County (392–3780); the **Edwin Booth Theater,** Harford Community College, Bel Air (838–1000).

MARYLAND'S EASTERN SHORE

Everywhere you look on Maryland's Eastern Shore there is a point jutting out into the Bay, a marshy creek providing a home to geese and ducks, old Southern mansions, wildflowers, and piney woods. This is pure Chesapeake Bay country and it is fascinating and relaxing to explore.

It is a particularly quiet place, removed geographically and historically from the motion of the Upper Bay and the Baltimore region but retaining its own history, which in fact predates much of its better-known neighbors to the west and north. Its flat terrain and sandy soil, its pace, and its woods, remind one of the South, as do its many small towns and fishing communities. It can be a hard place for those who live there, and there are the problems of poverty in some Eastern Shore rural areas. But the area is making a comeback, and tourism—with all

80

the amenities for tourists and boating afficionados—is increasingly an important part of the region's economy.

The Bay has created a dramatic but gentle coastline, leaving a scattering of islands—many of which can be visited and explored—and a ragged mass of quiet inlets and wet marshes, many of which can be sailed or fished or hunted. Crabbing and fresh- or salt-water fishing are easily learned and the end result, especially a Bay crab smothered in hot sauce and steamed until a fiery red, is delicious. This place is the home of Maryland's grandest tree—the 95-foot Wye Oak—and its most noble canine, the Chesapeake Bay retriever, Maryland's state dog.

As in the Upper Bay, the clearest guide to the Eastern Shore is by county, and it is county by county that we will explore Maryland's Eastern Shore.

Queen Anne's County

The Bay Bridge slopes gently into Queen Anne's County and travelers to seashore resorts in Maryland and Delaware whiz past. But away from the main highways a visitor can find a simple and relaxing county with an unusually unbroken view of the sky and with an almost constant breeze from the Bay.

The southern end of Kent Island was the site of the first settlement in Maryland. This is where William Claiborne established his fort and trading post in 1631. Centreville, the county seat, remains a good example of the sleepy Southern village/county seat, complete with a statue of Queen Anne on the green.

Talbot County

Talbot is a much busier but no less attractive county than Queen Anne's, its neighbor to the north. Its county seat, Easton, toots its horn as the "shopping center for the entire Eastern Shore." St. Michaels, a natural harbor and haven for boats, is becoming a popular stopover point for cruising boaters and motoring tourists. St. Michaels has a number of good restaurants. While the harbor, Chesapeake Bay Maritime Museum, and its restaurants attract increasing numbers of visitors each year, this old Bay port has managed to retain—even enhance—much of its former charm. The county's historic and deeply felt connection with the Bay is understandable since it claims that Talbot's 602 miles of waterfront is the most of any county in continental United States.

Tidal streams have created a long series of "necks," and most every neck is the site of an old mansion, a picturesque village, or more recently, a busy marina.

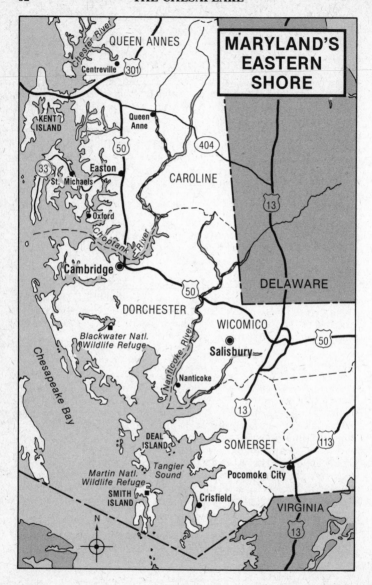

Dorchester County

South of Talbot, Dorchester, like the other Eastern Shore counties, is steeped in its own quiet history. It is home to the oldest Episcopal church in continous use in the United States. Cambridge is an attractive town that has links to the earliest settlers in the colonies. The county has numerous and longstanding fishing communities, and shares with Talbot County the Choptank River, setting for much of James Michener's *Chesapeake.* Indian lore has always been part of the county's heritage and many of its geographical names can be traced to the tribes that once hunted, fished, and lived on and around these shores. Dorchester is the largest county on the Eastern Shore, and probably has more marsh than any other. The county's marshland includes the Blackwater National Wildlife Refuge, which is nestled among wetland marshes such as Kentuck Swamp and Raccoon Creek and is home during the fall migrations to an estimated 80,000 Canada geese and 30,000 ducks.

Caroline County

Caroline has been referred to as the "inland county," although this is not totally accurate since the Choptank runs through it to the Bay. But, with its back against the Delaware state line, it does lack frontage on the Bay. While its commerce is therefore not particularly water-related, it does boast good bass fishing in the Choptank. Caroline's strength lies in being "a green place," and so it calls itself. This is a farming county that is blessed with good soil. The county is known for its tomatoes, canteloupes, and watermelon. It is proud of its simple way of life, its lack of great amusement parks or major tourist areas, even its lack of spectacular geography. It does, however, stress its large number of parks, campgrounds, and fishing and canoeing locations.

Wicomico County

Also linked closely with the Indians—its name comes from the tribe that once lived there—Wicomico County is the youngest of Maryland's counties, having been created in 1867. But Salisbury, the county's and the entire lower Shore's major center of commerce, was founded in 1732. Salisbury has restored many of is historic homes and other sites while retaining its place as a hub of the poultry, farming, and finance industries of the Shore.

Somerset County

Resting on the Virginia line, Somerset County and the nearby Bay islands remain as tightly involved with the Bay as they did when John Smith first visited and admired this part of the Bay in 1608. Workboats, including the Chesapeake's famous skipjacks—oyster boats powered by sail—still ply the waters, and Crisfield is known, and not just by its local boosters, as the "Seafood Capital of the World." Princess Anne, the county seat, is considered one of the most charming towns on the Shore. Life can be tough in a county that is so closely tied to the vagaries of the weather and water, but the people who live in Somerset have long been known to be a sturdy and persistent group. Nearby Smith and Deal Islands, perfect examples of fishing towns and life on the water, can be visited.

PRACTICAL INFORMATION FOR
MARYLAND'S EASTERN SHORE

PLACES TO STAY

HOTELS, MOTELS, AND INNS. Lodging on the Eastern Shore ranges from the small roadside motel—not always charming but usually clean and reasonable in price—to restored historic hotels and inns in some of the towns. Off-season rates, weekend rates, and special package deals are sometimes available. Bed and breakfast establishments are included in this list. There are several registries of accommodations in homes, yachts, and inns: Amananda's Bed and Breakfast, Ltd., P.O. Box 42, Long Green, MD 21092, 665–1333; and The Maryland Registry, c/o Sharp-Adams, Inc., 33 West St., Annapolis, MD 21401, 269–6232.

The following rates are based on double-occupancy during the usual tourist season: *Expensive,* $75 and up; *Moderate,* $40–$75; *Inexpensive,* $40 and under.

Queen Anne's County

Holly's Restaurant and Motel. *Inexpensive.* US 301 and US 50 (827–8711). Restaurant. A good location for visitors heading south.

Talbot County

Econo Lodge. US 50 in Easton (822–6330). *Inexpensive.* Restaurant nearby.

Harrison's Country Inn and Sportfishing Center. *Inexpensive.* Main St., Tilghman (886–2121). Live entertainment, outdoor pool.

Kemp House Smithton Inn. *Moderate.* 412 Talbot St., St. Michaels (745–2243). A B&B, with restaurant nearby and bikes for rent.

The Inn at Perry Cabin. *Expensive.* Rt. 33, St. Michaels (745–5178). Three dining rooms with good view of Miles River. Includes Continental breakfast. AE, MC, V.

1876 House. *Expensive.* 110 Morris St., Oxford (226–5496). A B&B with tennis, boating, and golf. Restaurant nearby.

Martingham Harbourtowne Inn. *Moderate.* St. Michaels (745–9066). Outdoor pool, tennis, golf, and restaurant.

Robert Morris Inn. *Moderate to expensive.* A gracious and attractive old inn. The Strand, Oxford (226–5111). Excellent restaurant, no TV or phones.

St. Michaels Motor Inn. Rt. 33 and Peaneck Road, St. Michaels (745–3333). Outdoor pool, coffee shop.

The Tidewater Inn. *Moderate.* Dover and Harrison Sts., Easton (822–1300). Live entertainment, outdoor pool, and fine dining room and restaurant. The Tidewater is one of the better-known longtime Eastern Shore establishments. Room service 7 A.M.–8 P.M. Free airport bus. Golf privileges. AE, CB, DC, MC, V.

Weaver's Inn. *Moderate.* 131 N. Washington St., Easton (822–1201). A B&B in one of the older buildings in town.

Dorchester County

The Governors Ordinary. *Moderate.* Water and Church Sts., Vienna (376–3530). A three-room B&B with restaurant, tennis, and boat ramp nearby.

Naticoke Manor House. *Moderate.* Church and Water Sts., Vienna (376–3530). Restaurant, tennis, and boating nearby.

Sarke Plantation. *Moderate.* Todd Point Rd., Cambridge (228–7020). A 3-room B&B in a country home with poolroom.

Quality Inn. *Moderate.* US 50, Cambridge (228–6900). Outdoor pool and restaurant. AE, CB, DC, MC, V.

Caroline County

The Sophie Kerr House. *Inexpensive.* 5th St. and Kerr Ave., Denton (479–3421). A B&B-style establishment with indoor pool, biking, badminton, and croquet. Its 5 rooms make it the largest inn in the county.

Wicomico County

Days Inn. *Inexpensive.* US 13 and Rt. 6, Salisbury (749–6200). Outdoor pool and playground. Restaurant nearby.

Holiday Inn. *Moderate.* US 13 N., Salisbury (742–7194). Live entertainment, outdoor pool, and restaurant. AE, CB, DC, MC, V.

Sheraton Salisbury Inn. *Moderate to expensive.* 300 S. Salisbury Blvd. (US 13), Salisbury (546–4400). Live entertainment, indoor pool, restaurant, and gym. Bar. AE, CD, DC, MC, V.

Somerset County

Frances Kitching's. *Moderate.* Ewell, Smith Island (425–3321). A 5-room B&B. Dinner and breakfast included. Open April to November.

Bernice Guy. *Moderate.* Ewell, Smith Island (425–2751). Small B&B with dinner and breakfast included. Closed in the winter.

The Pines Motel. *Inexpensive.* Somerset Ave., Crisfield (968–0900). Outdoor pool. Restaurant nearby.

Washington Hotel Inn. *Inexpensive.* Somerset Ave., Princess Ann (651–2525). A 10-unit hotel with restaurant and meeting rooms.

PLACES TO EAT

RESTAURANTS. Expect lots of crab dishes, fish, and fresh vegetables, all done in the simple but extremely tasty Eastern Shore manner. From the water to the kitchen is only a short distance, and much of the menu will vary with the catch of the day. Crab cakes and Imperial crab—a rich mixture of crabs, mayonnaise, and spices—are available at most eateries. Eating hardshelled crabs is messy—mounds of the tasty creatures on a newspaper on the table, accompanied by a pitcher of beer and cole slaw. Locals will sometimes race to see who can dismantle a crab the quickest, a wonder to behold as you slowly crack and claw your way through the meal. But don't fret. This is all part of the fun, and the taste of freshly steamed crab, or grilled oysters, or steamed clams, is worth the time and the trouble.

The cost of an à la carte dinner is the basis of our price range: *Expensive,* $25 and up; *Moderate,* $14–$25; *Inexpensive,* under $14.

Queen Anne's County

Hemingway's. *Moderate.* At the eastern foot of the Bay Bridge on US 50. Comfortable setting with a good view of the bridge and a professionally done menu of seafood, beef, and locally made desserts.

Talbot County

The Crab Claw Restaurant. *Moderate.* Navy Point, St. Michaels (745–2900). Steamed crabs ("if he don't kick we don't cook"—meaning they're *fresh*), cold beer and mixed drinks and a full menu besides. Oysters and clams in all sorts of ways—steamed, fried, and casinoed.

The Inn at Perry Cabin. *Moderate to Expensive.* Rt. 33, St. Michaels (745–5178). Seafood, veal, steak, and lamb in a pleasant, water setting at Fogg Cove. AE, MC, V.

Longfellows. *Moderate.* 125 Mulberry St., St. Michaels (745–2624). Harbor setting in a friendly restaurant frequented by the boating crowd. Fried oysters, crab dishes, and catch of the day. Also beef.

Martingham Harbourtowne Inn. *Moderate to expensive.* Rt. 33, St. Michaels. Sautéed veal in a fairly fancy setting. Also seafood in interesting, sometimes Continental, ways.

St. Michaels Inn. *Moderate to expensive.* Talbot Street, St. Michaels (745–3303). Seafood and Continental offerings in an inn-like setting.

Tidewater Inn. *Moderate.* Dover and Harrison Sts., Easton. (822–1300). Long known by locals and regular visitors for its solid and tasty fare, ranging from seafood to poultry to beef. AE, MC, V.

Dorchester County

Cater House. *Moderate.* 411 Muse St., Cambridge (221–0300). In a Victorian mansion, known for its local seafood dishes plus a Continental touch. Casual enough for the boating crowd.

Clayton's. *Moderate.* On the creek on Commerce St., Cambridge (228–7200). Steamed crabs as well as other seafood and meat dishes.

East Side Seafood Co. *Moderate.* At the foot of the bridge on Maryland Ave., Cambridge (228–9007). As the name says, fresh seafood dishes done in the Eastern Shore manner.

Caroline County

Melvin House. *Moderate.* On the green in Denton, Rt. 404 (479–1513). Family-run French restaurant with a menu that uses the local vegetables and fish.

Wicomico County

Christopher's on the Plaza. *Moderate.* Downtown Plaza, Salisbury (546–3104). Tableside cooking, surf and turf, veal and steaks.

Royal Exchange Pub. *Moderate.* S. Salisbury Avenue, Salisbury (749–1263). Continental style dining and menu plus freshly baked desserts and bread.

Somerset County

Auntem's. *Inexpensive.* Main St., Crisfield (968–0353). Known for its crab cakes, done in the meaty Eastern Shore style, and other seafood.

Frances Kitching's. *Inexpensive.* Ewell, Smith Island (425–3321). A family-style, simple but tasty menu relying heavily on the catch of the day.

Washington Hotel Inn Restaurant. *Moderate.* Washington Hotel Inn, Somerset Ave., Princess Anne. Seafood and shrimp platters.

BOATING. Perhaps most popular among Chesapeake boaters, the Eastern Shore of the Bay offers countless inlets and rivers to sail and explore. "Boating" is spoken here by just about everyone, and the area is a favorite for cross-Bay trips out of Annapolis or Baltimore.

There are simply too many marinas and rental/charter companies to list, but after selecting the area you wish to visit, you can call the following numbers for more extensive information: Queen Anne's, Caroline, and Talbot, 758–2300; Talbot County, 822–4606; Dorchester, 228–3234; Caroline, 758–3575; Wicomico, 546–3466; or Somerset, 651–2968.

Most marinas in the area monitor Channel 16.

HOW TO GET AROUND. Baltimore-Washington International Airport, south of Baltimore, is little more than an hour and a half, at the most, from most parts of the Eastern Shore. The Easton Airport is linked by regular flights to BWI. Also, Washington's National Airport is about an hour's drive from the Bay Bridge via US 50.

The Eastern Shore begins at the Bay Bridge (toll: $1.25 each way) and shortly after the bridge you may choose US 50, which swings south and parallels the Bay before turning east toward the ocean; US 301, which runs northeast into the farmland of the Upper Bay; or State Rt. 404, which cuts through the heart of the Eastern Shore on the way to the Delaware ocean resorts.

CRUISES AND TOURS. Walking and driving tours are available at most of the county tourism offices: **Queen Anne's, Caroline,** and **Talbot:** Tourism Council of the Upper Chesapeake, P.O. Box 66, Centreville, MD 21617, 758–2300; **Dorchester,** Dorchester County Tourism, P.O. Box 307, Cambridge, MD 21613, 228–3234; **Wicomico,** Convention and Visitors Bureau, Civic Center, Glen Ave. Extended, Salisbury, MD 21801, 546–3466; **Somerset,** Somerset County Tourism Commission, P.O. Box 243, Princess Anne, MD, 651–2968.

Cruises include Chesapeake Travel and Tours, a wide variety of land and water tours, 822–4383; Capt. Jason, Crisfield to Smith Island, 425–2351 or 425–5421; Capt. Tyler, Crisfield to Smith Island, can include lunch and bus tour, 425–2771; *Island Belle II,* Crisfield to Smith Island, 425–5431; *The Patriot,* Bay cruises, 745–5003; Steven Thomas, Tangier Island, VA, Crisfield, 968–2338; *Teresa Ann Evans,* Crisfield-Smith Island, 425–2201; *Teresa Ann,* Bay crusies from Reedville, VA, 804–453–3430. Most towns have local rental agencies for small boats and stores for a visitor's nautical needs.

THINGS TO SEE AND DO

Queen Anne's Courthouse and **Statue of Queen Anne,** 122 N. Commerce St., Centreville. One of two 18th-Century courthouses in Maryland, with a statue of the queen on the green.

Queen Anne's Courthouse, at Queenstown, Rt. 18 off US 301 (872–8088). Old courthouse and jail, dating back to 1708. Open summer, Sat. and Sun. 1–4. Free.

Tucker House, 124 S. Commerce St., Centreville (758–1347). Houses local historical society museum. Summer Fridays, noon–4. Small admission fee.

Wright's Chance, 119 S. Commerce St., Centreville (758–1347). Noted for its original wood paneling, dating from 1681. Summer Fridays, noon–4.

Talbot County

Customs House, Morris St. and the Strand, Oxford (226–5122). Replica of first U.S. Customs House. Free.

St. Michaels. Known as the birthplace of the Baltimore Clipper sailing sloop, this town—now spruced up and increasingly a popular stopover for tourists—provides lodging, restaurants, and historical exhibits. A pleasant harbor town for browsing.

Chesapeake Bay Maritime Museum. Maritime Rd., St. Michaels Harbor (745–2916). Floating collection of Chesapeake Bay working boats, and Bay and nautical history. Hooper Straight Lighthouse is a focal point. Gift shop. Tues.–Sun., summer 10–5, rest of year 10–4. Small admission fee.

Historical Society of Talbot County Museum. 25 S. Washington St., Easton (822–0773). Several changing exhibits, Federal townhouse (1810) and frame cottage (1797). Gardens and tours. Tues.–Sat. 10–4. Sun. 1–4. Small admission fee.

Oxford Museum. Morris and Market Sts., Oxford (226–5122). Local exhibits on this charming old maritime town. Hours vary. Donation.

St. Mary's Square Museum. At "The Green" in St. Michaels (745–9561). Local exhibits. Small admission fee.

Third Haven Meeting House. S. Washington St., Easton (822–0293). Perhaps the oldest frame building for religious services in United States. William Penn preached there and Lord Baltimore attended services. See caretaker for tour. Free.

Tilghman Island. On Rt. 33. Typical Chesapeake fishing town and home port to large portion of state's skipjack fleet.

Tred Avon (Oxford-Bellevue) Ferry. Oxford and Bellevue, (226–5408). Oldest "free running" ferry in United States. Sunrise to sunset. Toll.

Wye Church, Wye Mill, and Wye Oak. Wye Mills. Wye Church is one of the oldest Episcopal churches in America (Call 827–8853 for hours. Free). The Mill (827–8009) ground flour for Washington's army and still produces meal; summer, daily 9–5, winter Fri.–Sun., 9–5; donation. The mighty Wye Oak is the state's official state tree and is more than 400 years old. Free.

Dorchester County

Becky Phipps Cannon, Taylor's Island. During the War of 1812, the British blockaded the Bay, captured Maryland ships, and seized livestock and crops.

But when the ice jammed a British ship in the Choptank, the island militia seized a British landing party and this 12-pound cannon.

Cambridge. This old Eastern Shore tidewater town provides walking tours (guides available at the county office building at the foot of Court Lane, 228–3234). The tours take you among some of the oldest homes and streets on the Shore, and the guide explains the various architectural styles.

East New Market. Rt. 14 off Rt. 392. This community was settled in 1660. It includes many old homes, and a tour guide explaining the history of the houses and the town. East New Market was a supply center for the Continental Army. For information: 228–7953.

Meredith House. LaGrange Ave., Cambridge (228–7953 or 228–1102). Exhibits of seven Maryland governors, a farm museum, and a smoke house from the early 1700s. Small admission fee.

Dorchester Heritage Museum. Horn Point (228–4924). Contains maritime, aircraft, farming, and naturalist exhibits. Also contains exhibits of Indian life. Sat.–Sun., 1–4:30. Free.

Blackwater National Wildlife Refuge. Key Wallace Dr. off Rt. 335, Church Creek (228–2677). Massive and beautiful flocks of Canada geese rest and feed here in the late fall. Mid-October to mid-March is considered the best time to observe the birds that winter in these marshes. Besides the geese, the birds include whistling swans and more than 20 species of duck. Resident birds include some geese, ducks, the great blue heron, and the bald eagle, for whom the area ranks second only to Florida as a nesting place in the eastern United States. The mammals of Blackwater include the red fox, muskrat, deer, and several variaties of squirrel. Facilities offered are a visitor center with exhibits, a "wildlife drive" along the marshes, walking trails, a bike route, and fishing and boating. Visitor center is open daily 7:30–4, closed weekends in June, July, and August.

Old Trinity Church. Rt. 16 near Church Creek (228–2940). Dating from 1675, it is said to be the oldest Protestant church still in active use in the United States. Hours vary. Free.

South Dorchester County. Take Rt. 16 off US 50 to Rt. 335 and 336. This part of Dorchester has been called "the Cape Cod of the South." Picturesque, with small watermen's villages.

Spocott Windmill. Rt. 343, 6 miles west of Cambridge (228–7090). The original post windmill, used for grinding grain, was built in 1850 but destroyed in the awful blizzard of 1880. The present structure was erected in 1971 and is still operated in mild winds. Visible at all times. Free.

Vienna. US 50 and the Nanticoke River. Founded in 1700, this town probably got its name from the "emperor" of the Nanticoke Indians, Vinnacokasimmon. Historic homes along Water St. include the home of Gov. Thomas Holliday Hicks, who defeated legislators who wanted to join the Confederacy.

Caroline County

Caroline Farmers Market. Courthouse green, Denton, where farmers show off and sell their best. Spring to fall, Fri., 1–7; Sun. 11–3.

Choptank. Off Rt. 16. A small fishing town where you can fish and crab.

Mason-Dixon Crownstone. Marydel. Elaborately carved limestome post with the coats of arms of Lord Baltimore and William Penn. Free.

Pungy Wreck and George Martinak Cabin. Martinak State Park, Denton (479–1619). Skeleton of old-fashioned sailing vessel from Watts Creek. The cabin exhibits local memorabilia. Daily. Free.

Wicomico County

Mardela Springs. US 50 at Mardela. Famous 19th Century mineral springs. Free.

Mason-Dixon Marker. Rt. 54 near Mardela Springs. Eastern end of the north-south line of the Mason and Dixon boundary. Surveyed to settle fuss between Penn and Calvert families.

Newton Historic District. Elizabeth St. and Poplar Hill Ave., Salisbury (546–3466). Includes Poplar Hill mansion, oldest building in the city, and a group of Victorian homes built after the 1886 fire.

Pemberton Hall. Pemberton Dr., Salisbury (546–3466). Built in 1741 by Isaac Handy, the founder of Salisbury. Historic park on its 61 acres. Sun. 1–3. Donation.

Poplar Hill Mansion. 117 Elizabeth St., Salisbury (749–1776). Renowned architectural work, especially the cornices. Sun. 1–4. Free.

Whitehaven and Whitehaven Ferry. Off Rt. 352. Oldest town on Wicomico River and once an important port and shipbuilding center. Washington's grandmother is believed to have lived here. The ferry carries passengers and cars across river during daylight hours. Free.

Wildfowl Carving and Art Museum. Holloway Hall, Salisbury State College, Rt. 13, Salisbury (742–4988). Famous exhibits of bird carvings and antique decoys. Daily, 10–5. Small admission fee.

Salisbury Zoo. Memorial Pl. and Park Dr., Salisbury (742–2123). More than 400 reptiles, birds, and mammals, including Spectacled Bears, jaguars, and bison.

Somerset County

Crisfield. Rt. 413. The self-proclaimed—not inaccurately—"Seafood Capital of the World." The city dock is the site of packing plants, oyster dredge repair shops, and a crab barrel factory.

Deal Island. Rt. 363 off US 13. Small watermen's village where skipjacks can be seen before the oystering season.

Princess Anne. Rt. 388. Princess Anne's historic district includes the Manokin Presbyterian Church (1765), Tunstall Cottage (1733), and St. Andrews Episcopal Church (1770).

Smith Island. Tangier Sound in the Bay (651–2968). Laced with canals, this is the Eastern Shore in all its beauty and hard work. About 800 persons live on the island, which can be reached only by boat (see Cruises). The island is named for Captain John Smith, who first saw it in 1608.

Teackle Mansion. Prince William St., Princess Anne (651–2968). Replica of Scottish manor house built in 1802. Sun., 2–4. Small admission fee.

Crisfield Historical Museum. Main St., Crisfield (968–2390). From Indian times to the present. A good, full look at the history of life on and near the water. Mon.–Sat., 10:30–12:15 and 1:30–5. Free.

Eastern Shore Early Americana Museum. Hudsons Corner (623–8324). Old poultry house includes rural exhibits from 1750 to the present. Thurs.–Sun., 10–5. Small admission fee.

Lem Ward Museum. City Dock, Crisfield (968–2500). Carvings and paintings by the well-known waterfowl artists, Steve and Lem Ward. Daily, 9–5. Small admission fee.

FISHING. You don't have to be an expert fisherman or hunter to enjoy the Shore's unique and bountiful opportunities. Fishing and crabbing sites are available in almost every tidewater town off almost every bridge and along each shore. You are permitted to catch up to one bushel of crabs per day. Methods include simply dipping the net in the water and hoping you see a crab to chase and catch. Most crabbers use bait (usually chicken necks or fish heads) on the end of a line. The crab will approach the bait slowly and if you're careful can be coaxed within the range of your long-handled net. Traps are also used and are available at many local fishing stores, as are nets, steaming pots, and friendly expert advice.

Most of the purely fresh water fishing on the Shore is in ponds and the upper reaches of the many streams and rivers. Trout and bass are stocked. Caroline County offers several fresh water fishing sites (Tourism Council of the Upper Chesapeake, P.O. Box 66, Centreville, MD 21617, 758–2300).

Bay fish include black drum, channel bass, flounder, blue fish, perch, and weakfish. Tidewater rivers—the Choptank, Nanticoke, Pocomoke, and Wicomico—are home to the largemouth bass, bluegill, and other species. Licenses are required for most areas. Write the Department of Natural Resources, Licensing and Consumer Services, Tawes State Office Building, Annapolis, MD 21401 (269–3765) for complete information.

For information about charter boats call or write the Tourism Council of the Upper Bay, P.O. Box 66, Centreville, MD 21617 (758–2300); or Somerset County Tourism Commission, P.O. Box 243, Princess Anne, MD 21853 (651–2968).

HUNTING. Hunting geese and ducks is a major sport on the Eastern Shore, which lies at the heart of the Atlantic Flyway. Quail and deer are also popular targets. The regulations for hunting—as for fishing—are strict and detailed. For more information, write or call the Department of Natural Resources, Licensing and Consumer Services, Tawes State Office Building, Annapolis, MD 21401 (269–3765).

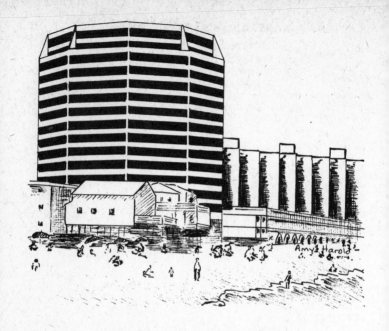

Amy & Harold

OCEAN CITY AND
WORCESTER COUNTY

Although Ocean City isn't actually *on* Chesapeake Bay, Maryland's Atlantic Ocean resort and the state's easternmost county lie well within the Chesapeake Vacationland.

Ocean City is sun, sand, surf, and sky—a salt-air mecca of sun-washed days and soft summer nights, soaring gulls and sauntering bikinis, sandcastles, beach cottages, high-rise hotels and condominiums.

Inland from Ocean City (and Assateague Island to the south), Worcester County is a haven of rural tranquility—picturesque Snow Hill and Pokomoke City, farmland, river, and natural forest.

Most visitors will enter Worcester County by car: US 113 or Route 528 south from Delaware; US 50, east from Salisbury to Ocean City; State Route 12 between Salisbury and Snow Hill, or US 13, south from

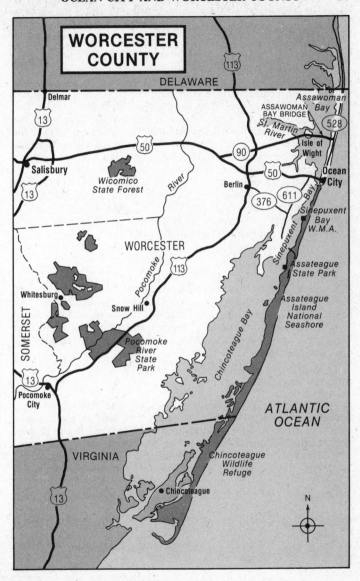

Salisbury or north from Norfolk, Virginia. But because Ocean City is the focal point, this chapter will explore Worcester County outward from the coast.

Ocean City

Built along a barrier strip of sand that is often only two blocks wide, Ocean City stretches south from the Delaware state line for more than 150 city blocks. Blessed with almost 10 miles of sandy ocean beach, the city looks eastward toward the Atlantic and westward toward the mainland over a series of picturesque and protected bays—Montego, Big Assawoman, Isle of Wight, and Sinepuxent. The bays and the city's commercial boat harbor are open to the ocean through the Inlet between Ocean City and Assateague Island to the south. The Ocean City boardwalk fronts on the ocean between the Inlet and 28th Street. Motorists enter Ocean City via the Coastal Highway (Rt. 528) from the north (Delaware), the Assawoman Bay Bridge (Rt. 90 at 62nd Street), or US 50 near the heart of Ocean City's Old Town.

Assateague Island

Assateague Island, like Ocean City, is a barrier strip of seashore and a major touring destination—but the similarity between the two stops there. Each has more than a fair share of sun, sand, and surf, but if Ocean City is a wonderland of beach bunnies and boardwalk fun, Assateague is the lovely and natural home of the Assateague pony, the tern, and the gull.

North Assateague

North Assateague is the Maryland section of the island and is easily accessible by car from Ocean City. Take US 50 west for about a mile, then turn left on Route 611 (south) and watch for the left turn (a short distance past Frontier Town) over the New Bridge to Assateague Island. The National Park Service has a headquarters and maintains a Visitor's Center (on your right) shortly before you cross the bridge over Sinepuxent Bay to Assateague. North Assateague is divided into three parts: six sandy miles of "wild" beach, accessible only on foot, on your left as you drive onto the island; Assateague State Park in the midsection; and, to the south, Assateague Island National Seashore, another natural expanse of surf and sandy dunes. There is a State Park Information Center (with campground registration) on your left near the park end of Sinepuxent Bay Bridge.

And now, a word about those free spirits of the seashore—Assateague's famous ponies: They may look gentle, and usually they are, but they're also unpredictable—they kick and sometimes they bite. It's really hard to blame them, considering the fact that their forebearers swam ashore from a foundering Spanish galleon in the 16th Century and they've been munching on marsh grass and bayberry leaves ever since.

There are two herds of Assateague ponies on the island, a larger group in the Virginia section to the south, and a smaller herd in Maryland. Virginia's Chincoteague Volunteer Fire Department owns the southern ponies and manages an annual July roundup and auction; the National Park Service manages Maryland's Assateague's wild pony herd.

PRACTICAL INFORMATION
FOR OCEAN CITY
AND WORCESTER COUNTY

PLACES TO STAY

HOTELS AND MOTELS. Ocean City is a seaside resort, worshiping the sun in the summer, but attracting an increasing number of visitors during the balmy days of spring, the crisp days of autumn, and even the quiet months of winter. Room rates in the following selection of accommodations will vary widely between summer and winter, and our prices, when given, are intended merely as a guide. If possible, call or write before you commit yourself. If this isn't possible, pin down the price before you sign in, perhaps even request to see the unit or room. Finally, keep in mind that this is a *selection* only, and we can't include all of the many excellent accommodations in the Ocean City resort area.

Sheraton Fontainebleau Inn & Spa. *Deluxe.* 101st St. and 10100 Ocean Hwy., 21842; 524–3535 or (800) 325–3535. 228 rooms and 22 suites, most with an ocean view. Full-service restaurant and cocktail lounge. Heated indoor pool and fully equipped health spa. AE, CB, DC, MC, V.

Spinnaker Motel. *Moderate to Expensive.* 18th St. and Oceanside, 21842; 289–5444 or (800) 638–3244. 100 rooms, all units with kitchens. Private balconies with ocean views. Heated outdoor pool with sundeck. Coffee shop. AE, MC, V.

Carousel Hotel. *Deluxe.* 118th St., on the Beach, 21842; 524–1000 or (800) 641–0011. 240 rooms, 15 suites, with June to September rates higher. Some suites. Two restaurants, two cocktail lounges, open year round. AE, CB, DC, MC, V.

Holiday Inn-Ocean Front. *Moderate to Expensive.* 67th St. and Ocean Front, 21842; 524–1600 or (800) HOLIDAY. 217 rooms, open year round. Indoor/outdoor pool. Restaurant and lounge. AE, CB, DC, MC, V.

The Dunes Motel. *Moderate.* 27th St. and Beach, 21842; 289–4414. 104 rooms, February till October 27. Efficiency oceanfront units. Food only. Outdoor pool. AE, MC, V.

Best Western Flagship Ocean Front. *Moderate to Expensive.* Boardwalk and 26th St., 21842; 289–3384 or (800) 528–1234. 93 rooms. Jonah and the Whale Seafood Buffet. The Flagship is on the ocean. AE, CB, DC, MC, V.

Phillips Beach Plaza Hotel. *Moderate to Expensive.* Oceanfront at 13th St., 21842; 289–9121. 86 rooms Phillips-by-the-Sea Restaurant. Cocktail lounge and Beach Plaza Cafe. Open all year. AE, CB, DC, MC, V.

Quality Inn-Ocean Front. *Moderate to Expensive.* On the Oceanfront & 54th St., 21842; 524–7200 or (800) 228–5151. 130 rooms. Year-round inn with 5-story plant-filled atrium. Atrium Cafe. AE, CB, DC, MC, V.

Qualtiy Inn-Boardwalk. *Expensive.* Boardwalk at 17th St., 21842; 289–4401 or (800) 228–5151. 172 rooms. All efficiencies, with honeymoon suites. Food only. AE, CB, DC, MC, V.

Santa Maria Motor Hotel. *Moderate.* 1500 Baltimore Avenue, Box 400, 21842 (15th and Boardwalk); 289–7191. 102 rooms. Full-service restaurant. 30 rooms facing the ocean. Balconies. MC, V.

Beachmark Motel. 7300 Coastal Hwy., 21842; 524–7300 or (800) 638–1600. 97 rooms, open May through mid-September. Fully equipped efficiencies, with coffee shop. Outdoor pool.

The Carriage House. *Moderate to Deluxe.* 29th St. and Baltimore Ave., 21842; 289–7291. 38 rooms, 42 apartments. Open April through October. Located on the oceanside in North Ocean City. June through August. Outdoor pool.

Commander Hotel. *Expensive.* 14th St. and Boardwalk, 21842; 281–6166. 103 rooms. Boardwalk Cabaret Dinner Theatre. Efficiency apartments July and August. Modified American Plan. Pool.

Fenwick Inn. *Expensive.* 138th St., 21842; 524–1100. 201 rooms in a year-round inn. Penthouse restaurant and lounge with nightly entertainment. Indoor heated pool.

Misty Harbor. *Inexpensive to Moderate.* 25th St. and Philadelphia Ave., 21842; 289–7284. 57 rooms, 26 apartments and efficiencies. Apartments $225 and up, July through Labor Day. Free rowboats.

Nassau Motel. 60th St. and Oceanside, 21842; 524–6200. 21 rooms, 41 efficiencies. April through October. Pool.

Riviera Motel. *Moderate.* 26th St. and Baltimore Ave., 21842; 289–6831. 63 rooms, March through October. Pool.

Sahara Motel. *Moderate.* 19th St. and Oceanfront, 21842; 289–8101. 113 rooms, mid-April through September. Poolside, oceanview, and oceanfront rooms. Pool.

Stowaway Americana Hotel. *Moderate to Expensive.* 22nd St. and Board-walk, 21842; 289–6191. 132 rooms, open year round. Pool and restaurant.

Surf and Sands Motel. *Moderate to Expensive.* 23rd St. and Boardwalk, 21842; 289–7161. 96 rooms, open Easter to October. Coffee shop, breakfast and lunch. Outdoor and heated kiddy pool.

PLACES TO EAT

RESTAURANTS AND CAFES. As is true with any popular resort city, visitors to Ocean City are faced with a happy but bewildering selection of places to eat—fast food to fabulous food, hot dogs to chateaubriand. The following selection of restaurants is not meant to be all-inclusive. We have attempted to include eating places that will appeal to a wide variety of tastes and pocketbooks—family groups to swinging singles, the inexpensive to the wildly extravagant. The editors would appreciate hearing of that "very special place" that you discover during your stay in Ocean City. If space permits, we will try to include it in future editions.

The Marina Deck. *Moderate.* 306 Dorchester St.; 289–4411. Fresh seafood, with a raw bar. Domestic wine list, but there's always that strawberry shortcake or pecan pie.

Phillips by the Sea. *Moderate.* Boardwalk and 13th St.; 289–9121. A "seafood adventure" in Phillips Beach Plaza Hotel, featuring crab cakes, crab claws, and steamed spiced shrimp. Also, **Phillips Crab House,** 289–6821, 21st St. and Philadelphia, casual and relaxed; and **Phillips Seafood House,** Philadelphia at 14th St., where seafood is a specialty, 542–9200. V, MC, AE.

Reflections. *Moderate to Expensive.* 67th St. and Coastal Highway; 524–5252. French-American cuisine in the European tradition. A respectable wine list, with local seafood, beef, and veal. Year round. Major credit cards.

Gringo's Restaurant & Cantina. *Inexpensive to Moderate.* 5309 Coastal Highway; 504–6244. Gringos are welcome at Gringo's. California-Mexican. Dinners 5 to 11 P.M., with late-night bites in Tio's Lounge. Major credit cards.

Angler. *Moderate.* Talbot St. and the Bay; 289–6980. Sit on the dock and enjoy the Bay. Fresh seafood daily, breakfast, lunch, and dinner. Reservations suggested.

Kate Bunting's. *Moderate.* 10 Talbot St.; 289–1441. Steamed crabs, lunch or dinner, inside or out; in a restored turn-of-the-century inn.

Mario's. *Moderate.* 22nd St. and Philadelphia Ave.; 289–9445. Continental menu, with a bar, and entertainment during summer season. Closed early December and Mondays during the winter. AE, MC, V.

Captain Bill Bunting's Angler. *Moderate.* Talbot St. & the Bay, 21842; 289–7424. Restaurant, patio bar, and marina, with "a free cruise with dinner." Early—5 A.M.!—breakfast for early risers. Tropical drinks. Reservations suggested.

Gold Coast Deli. *Inexpensive.* 115th St. and Coastal Highway—"Home of Mama Del Camp" in Gold Coast Mall; 723–DELI. Dine in or carry out.

Sandwiches, spaghetti, and bagels and lox, all in the $3 to $6 range. Beer and wine.

The Hobbit Restaurant and Bar. *Inexpensive to Moderate.* 81st St. and the Bay; 524-8100. Fish, fowl, and real francaise—all entrees served with Hobbit salad and fresh-baked bread. MC, V.

Fager's Island. *Moderate.* 60th St. in the Bay; 524–5500. Lunch and dinner, with a bar till 2 A.M. and a spacious outdoor deck. Spectacular sunsets on the quiet side of the beach. Entrees from traditional to exotic.

Peppermill's Paradise Cafe. *Moderate to Expensive.* 42nd St. and the Bay, a block north of the Convention Center; 289–4200. Continental and American cuisine in a casual bayfront atmosphere. Reservations accepted.

Weitzel's Restaurant. *Inexpensive to Moderate.* 51st St. and Coastal Hwy.; 524–6990. A family favorite, serving crab cakes and chicken, informal style. Also a carryout.

The Wharf. *Moderate to Expensive.* 128th St.; 524–1001. Seafood, veal, steaks, and chicken in a nautical atmosphere. Lounge with happy hour between 5 and 6 P.M. Adjacent to Wharf Seafood & Spirits Market. AE, MC, V.

Tony's Casa Di Pasta. *Moderate.* 33rd St. and Coastal Highway; 289–4588. A full Italian menu, with homemade pastas. Live entertainment in the Sandbar Lounge. Open at 4 P.M.

Harrison's Harbor Watch. *Inexpensive to Moderate.* Boardwalk South, overlooking the Inlet; 289–5121. A spectacular view and overstuffed sandwiches; fresh local seafood. Major credit cards.

Rayne's. *Inexpensive to Moderate.* 7 Dorchester St., just off Boardwalk; 289–9141. Breakfast, lunch, dinner, but noted for its Olde Fashioned Soda Fountain. Beer, on and off, with a carryout.

The Longhorn. *Moderate.* Boardwalk and 15th St.; 524–3229. A family steak house with reduced prices for children. Cocktails. Open May–September. Major credit cards.

Paul Revere Smorgasbord. *Moderate.* Boardwalk at 2nd St.; 524–1776. Roast beef, pork chops, chicken, and 100 other home-cooked entrees, including homemade bread and desserts. Children's prices. April through October. Major credit cards.

McGee's. *Moderate.* Boardwalk and 4th St.; 289–7181. An Irish pub and restaurant, with Irish entertainment.

THINGS TO SEE AND DO

THE BEACH. First there is the beach, then the Boardwalk, then the city, and finally the Bay. But it all starts at the beach, where Atlantic surf meets the shore. The beach is why it's all *there.* Ocean City's beaches, which fringe the ocean for ten sandy miles, lie totally within the city's limits, stretching northward from the Inlet to the Maryland–Delaware line. Sunbathing and swimming—or watching others sunbathe and swim—are the main beach pursuits, but designated sections of the beach have been set aside for fishing and surfboarding. If you've never splashed in salt water, ogled a bikini, listened to the racous cry of a gull, or helped a child build a sandcastle, don't worry—it's really easy; you'll catch on soon enough.

THE BOARDWALK. Ocean City is proud of its ocean boardwalk—and rightly so. Three miles long (the Inlet to 28th Street), the boardwalk is open 24 hours a day for strolling, jogging, and ocean or people watching. Bicyclists may use the boardwalk between 6 and 10 in the morning. The Boardwalk Train runs the length of the boardwalk every 20 minutes, Memorial Day through Labor Day. The fare is 75¢ one way, $1.50 round trip.

Ocean City Life Saving Station Museum. Located at the south end of the boardwalk, overlooking the Inlet, the Life Saving Station Museum traces Ocean City's history from its founding as a fishing village in the 1800s to the resort it is today. Housed in the former Life Saving Station, built in 1891, the museum is open daily from 11 A.M. to 10 P.M., June through September, and weekends the rest of the year. Adults $1.00, children 12 and under 50¢.

Jolly Roger. 30th St. off Ocean Highway. A family amusement complex, featuring a water slide, golf courses, driving range, major and kiddie rides, and mini-speed and bumper boats. Snacks are available. Open till 11 P.M.

OLD TOWN. "Downtown" Ocean City, bounded by South Second St. on the Inlet to 15th St. and the ocean to the bay, features Inlet Village with fine restaurants and shops, "the widest beach in town" on the ocean side, docks and fishing boats on the bayside, interesting shops, hotels, and restaurants throughout Old Town, and live and lively entertainment from Commander Boardwalk Cabaret (Ocean City's only professional theater, 14th St. and Boardwalk) and The Purple Moose Saloon (Boardwalk between Talbot and Carolina Sts.) for older folk to Marty's Playland, Timper Rides, and Bamboo Mini Golf for the younger crowd. And, for everyone, two favorites are Rayne's Olde Fashioned Soda Fountain (7 Dorchester St., just off the Boardwalk) or Zip's Happy Kid's, "the Original Make-Your-Own-Sundae" (203 N. Baltimore Ave. or Boardwalk near Division St.).

CRUISES. The following is a partial listing of evening, ocean, and bay cruises out of Ocean City. Times and destinations are subject to change, so call before making your plans. Boats include *Angler,* evening scenic cruises, 5, 7, and 9 P.M., Talbot St., 289–7424; *Bay Queen,* Assawoman Bay cruises, 10 A.M., noon, and 2 P.M., Talbot St. Pier, 289–9125; *Mariner,* Atlantic cruises, 6:30–8 P.M., Talbot St., 289–9125; *Starfish,* evening scenic cruises, Talbot St., 7:30 P.M., 289–8547; and *Taurus,* ocean cruises, Bahia Marina, Bay between 21st and 22nd Sts., 7:30 P.M., 289–7234.

SPORTFISHING. Ocean City is the White Marlin Capital of the World, and the Ocean City Marlin Club is one of the oldest fishing clubs in the country. The $30,000 White Marlin Open is held in mid-August, with the White Marlin Tournament following Labor Day Weekend. Outboard motor boats may be rented from marinas, six headboats sail early each morning for ocean fishing, and boats may be chartered with captain and mate. Some boats available are: *Pursuer,* a 42-footer, docked at Talboat Street Pier, 289–9125; *Liquidator,* 42 feet, 289–0828; and *Huntress,* 46 feet, 289–9461. The *Tortuga,* 24 passengers, and *Taylor Maid,* 78 passengers, operate out of Bahia Marina, on the Bay between 21st and 22nd Sts., 289–7438.

ANTIQUES & CRAFTS FLEA MARKET. Ocean City Convention Hall, 40th St. and Coastal Hwy., 289–8313. Open Friday, Saturday, and Sunday, 9 A.M. to 5 P.M. (if it doesn't rain), early May through mid-October, Ocean City's giant flea market features antiques, second-hand items, and handmade crafts.

On the Mainland—Worchester County

Frontier Town. Route 611, a short drive south of Ocean City; 289–7877. (Rt. 50, west one mile, then south a few miles on Rt. 611, Stephen Decatur Hwy.) The Wild, Wild West on the Eastern Shore—a family theme park with bank holdups, Indian dancers, gunfights, and cancan girls, plus rides on a riverboat, steam train, stagecoach, and ponies. Open daily during the summer, 10 A.M. to 6 P.M. One admission for all shows and rides. Light lunches at Longhorn and Golden Nugget Saloons.

OUTDOOR PARKS AND PICNIC AREAS. Shad Landing State Park, boating and picnicking on the Pocomoke River, Route 113 south of Snow Hill; **Milburn Landing State Park,** west bank of Pocomoke, Rt. 364, north of Pocomoke City; **Pocomoke State Forest,** deer hunting in season, Rt. 12, west of Snow Hill; **Byrd Park** in Snow Hill; **Stephen Decatur Park** in Berlin; **Pocomoke Cypress Swamps** (Pocomoke River State Park), accessible from Rt. 113, Pocomoke, and—of course—**Assateague Island State Park and National Seashore.**

HISTORIC SITES. Snow Hill. A charming and historic hamlet—and Worcester County seat—on the Pocomoke River, Rts. 12 and 394. Founded in 1642, Snow Hill was once a busy river port. The Julia A. Purnell Museum, 208 West Market St., is Snow Hill's showcase of Worcester County lore. The museum is open weekdays, 9 A.M. to 5 P.M., and weekends, 1 P.M. to 5 P.M.; (301) 632–0515. The Nassawango (Iron) Furnace, one of the oldest industrial sites in Maryland, has been registered as a National Historic Place and is being restored, Rt. 12, Old Furnace Rd., near Snow Hill.

Amy Harold

VIRGINIA'S EASTERN SHORE

Virginia's Eastern Shore, a 70-mile peninsula and secluded barrier islands, is one of the most fancifully beautiful places in America. It is a haven for herds of wild ponies. There are unspoiled beaches with rare and elaborate seashells, as well as charter boats to the islands, lazy lagoons, and quiet coves.

This is a region visited by Blackbeard the pirate and one adorned with romantic placenames such as Nassawodox, Kiptopeke, and Pungoteague. Even the familiar names are colorful: Temperanceville, Birdsnest, and Modest Town.

One side of Virginia's Eastern Shore is bathed by the Atlantic and the other by the Chesapeake Bay. This favored location guarantees the visitor a continuous feast of delicious and succulent seafood. There is even an annual local festival to honor it, with fresh oysters, fried eel, steamed clams, and chowder of unmatched quality and flavor.

The attractions of this area are unique and varied. Two of America's few preserved debtor's prisons are here, one at Eastville and one at

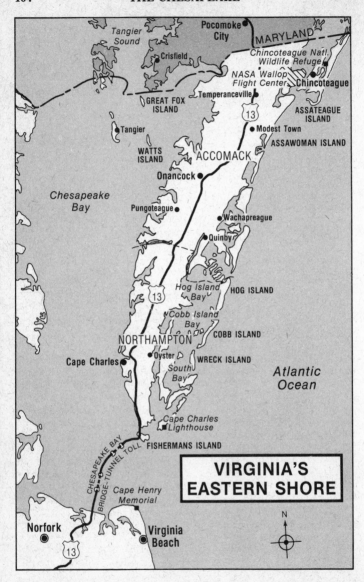

Tangier Sound

Pocomoke City

MARYLAND

Crisfield

Chincoteague Natl.
Wildlife Refuge

NASA Wallop
Flight Center

Chincoteague

GREAT FOX
ISLAND

Temperanceville

13

ASSATEAGUE
ISLAND

Tangier

Modest Town

WATTS
ISLAND

ASSAWOMAN ISLAND

ACCOMACK

Onancock

Chesapeake
Bay

Pungoteague

Wachapreague

Quinby

HOG ISLAND

Hog Island
Bay

Cobb Island
Bay

13

COBB ISLAND

NORTHAMPTON

Cape Charles

Oyster

WRECK ISLAND

Atlantic
Ocean

South
Bay

Cape Charles
Lighthouse

FISHERMANS ISLAND

CHESAPEAKE BAY

BRIDGE-TUNNEL TOLL

Cape Henry
Memorial

Norfork

Virginia
Beach

13

N

**VIRGINIA'S
EASTERN SHORE**

Accomack. Tiny Tangier Island, accessible only by boat, has residents who still speak Elizabethan dialect. At Chincoteague and Assateague, each summer brings the famous Wild Pony Roundup. This is a day of carnivals and shows, good food, and high spirits, a time to retell the fascinating legends about the island ponies, descendants of horses that swam ashore from a wrecked Spanish galleon centuries ago.

A trip to the Eastern Shore is not complete without a close look at some of the beautiful craftwork created here. Eastern Shore duck decoys for instance, are deservedly in demand nationwide. There is also excellent saltwater fishing here, as well as canoeing in the marshes and hiking everywhere. Some particularly lovely natural areas are in the Chincoteague National Wildlife Refuge. The vigilant observer can spot numerous marsh and water birds, rabbits, raccoons, deer otters, and muskrats.

Everywhere visitors go on Virginia's Eastern Shore they are aware of being in a very special and natural world. From the isolated fishing villages to the unspoiled beaches, this is what America was like in less complicated times when nature was untouched by progress.

EXPLORING VIRGINIA'S EASTERN SHORE

The 17.6-mile Chesapeake Bay Bridge-Tunnel deposits northbound visitors from Virginia Beach, Norfolk, and Williamsburg on the southern tip of Virginia's Eastern Shore. The views from this bridge are a delight. There is a scenic stop, restaurant, and a fishing pier with bait and tackle. Visitors can see both the Atlantic Ocean and Chesapeake Bay as they cross this engineering marvel to the quiet peninsula north of Norfolk. Dipping from the bridge into one of the tunnels and under a massive, oceangoing freighter will take some visitors' breath away.

Virginia's Eastern Shore is bounded on the east coast by the wetlands and barrier islands of the Atlantic Ocean, and on the west by Chesapeake Bay. It was first visited by Europeans in 1608 when an exploring party lead by Captain John Smith mapped the bayside and Chesapeake Islands. In 1614, the Jamestown government obtained the land from the Indians. The English came to the peninsula to stay in 1620. The settlement was called Accomack Plantation until 1634 when it became one of the eight original counties. In 1643, the name was changed to Northampton. Then, in 1663, the county was divided to form Accomack County in the north and Northampton County in the south. The area has been able to preserve much of its early charm because of the relative isolation it enjoyed until the Bay Bridge-Tunnel opened in 1965.

The people of Accomack organized early. There was a census in 1624, listing their names and ages, and the ships on which they had arrived. In these two counties can be found the earliest continuous court records in the United States, dating from 1632.

Among other things, the records tell of the trial and acquittal in the case of a play, "The Bear and the Cub," in 1665, giving the Eastern Shore the distinction of having the first record of a dramatic performance in America. Tours of the two county seats include the Debtors Prison in Accomack, and the Debtors Prison, Court House, and Clerk's Office in Eastville.

Eastern Shore architecture is unique. Most early dwellings now standing are of frame construction with varying roof levels and two or more chimneys. The roofs are mostly of the A-type with small dormer windows on the front and back. Other houses are two full stories, some all brick, some with brick ends and some all frame. A house with four different roof levels is often referred to as "big house, little house, colonnade, and kitchen." These houses can be explored all over the area.

Cape Charles

Cape Charles, where the Bay Bridge-Tunnel drops visitors, was established in 1884 when the New York, Philadelphia and Norfolk Railroad extended its service from Philadelphia to Norfolk. It is the largest town in Northampton County and offers excellent fishing, boating, and beaches. It is one of the few places on the East Coast where visitors can watch breathtaking sunsets over water.

Eyre Hall, for example, just south of Eastville, was built by Littleton Eyre in 1735 and has been in his family ever since. It boasts one of the oldest and loveliest boxwood gardens in America. It was enlarged by his son, Severn, in 1765 and furnished with handsome Queen Anne, Chippendale, and Hepplewhite pieces, family portraits, and Chinese Export. In the cross hall is an interesting scenic wallpaper in French block designed by duFour. Throughout the house are fine woodwork and paneling.

Eastville itself was not founded until 1766, but it has the distinction that its County Court declared the Stamp Act of Parliament unconstitutional. The old Courthouse in Eastville contains the oldest court records in the United States, the first legible date being January 7, 1632. The preservation and survival of these records is all the more remarkable because they were housed in the homes of the court clerks for more than 100 years. Other sights include a Debtor's Prison (1644), the

Clerk's Office (1719), the Court House (1730), and Parke Hall (1794). The nearby town of Oyster is famous for its seafood industries.

Historic Onancock

Still farther north and on the Bay, Onancock is the home of the Eastern Shore Historical Society, housed in Kerr Place, which was originally built in 1790. Onancock's large, deep harbor offers well protected docking facilities for pleasure craft of all sizes. The public dock and boat launching ramp are used by local and visiting sportsmen and commercial boats.

Historic sights in Onancock include the site of Fowkes' Tavern, home of the first play in America, and St. George's Episcopal Church, built in 1652. Sights from the 20th-Century include the Town of Willis Wharf with its seafood industries and fishing facilities and the Virginia Institute of Marine Sciences.

Within a short radius of Accomack, in the North, visitors will find more restored Colonial architecture than in any other place in the United States except Williamsburg. Individual houses, however, are not opened to the public except when advertised or for Historic Garden Week. Sights include The Glade, The Little House (ca. 1767), The Haven (1794), Ailworth House (1795), Roseland (1771), Seymour House and Ice House (1791), Court House Green and the Debtors' Prison (1782).

The Eastern Shore, however, relies for income less on tourism than on agriculture, the biggest industry. The two counties together produce a bounty on the 120,000 acres of cropland. The Eastern Shore leads the state in the production of vegetables. The Irish potato is the most important crop with 30,000 acres planted annually but corn and soybeans are fast growing in importance. Sweet potatoes, snapbeans, tomatoes, cucumbers, and peppers are grown. Whether passing through or spending a vacation, visitors will want to stop at the roadside stands to sample and purchase the luscious local produce. There are also almost 150,000 acres of beautiful forestlands with loblolly pine predominating.

More and more farmers are moving into the production of broilers and two processing plants for chickens are in Accomack County.

Another important source of income for the Shore is the seafood industry. This includes oysters, hard clams, sea clams, crab, and finfish. Oyster beds are cultivated on both bayside and seaside. Hard clams or quahog are in great quantity. The largest clam packing plant in the world is located on Chincoteague. The sea clam industry is new to the Shore where both blue and soft crabs are abundant. The finfish industry is based on some 40 different species.

Chincoteague

Chincoteague Island, Virginia's only resort island, is perhaps the most beautiful of the many islands that dot Virginia's Eastern Shore. World famous for its oyster beds and clam shoals, this picturesque island is the gateway to the National Seashore and Chincoteague Wildlife Refuge. This serene fishing settlement, seven miles long and 1½ miles wide, and abounding with history and natural beauty, welcomes visitors to explore its unique heritage.

The first Colonists were humble sailors and herders who arrived in the early 1670s. With the exception of salvaging shipwrecks off Assateague Island, the economy remained primarily farming and livestock. Today, however, the surrounding waters are the main source of local income.

The island's famous salt oysters, sold since 1830, are cultivated on leased "rock" and public grounds which the watermen seed and harvest. Chincoteague is the home of many outstanding craftsmen and artists who produce some of the world's finest hand-carved duck decoys and wildfowl wood carvings.

Assateague Island

Protecting Chincoteague Island from the Atlantic Ocean, Assateague Island boasts more than 37 miles of the widest and most beautiful beaches on the East Coast. This rare beauty is protected by the Assateague Island National Seashore and Chincoteague National Wildlife Refuge. A wide variety of nature activities and many miles of unspoiled beaches and sand dunes are there to explore.

Assateague Island is well-known as a birdwatcher's paradise. Over 260 species are to be found, and as the days get colder, the arrival of the Canadian geese and snow geese and the whistling voices of the swans herald the onset of winter.

The most popular inhabitants of the Refuge, however, are the Chincoteague wild ponies, made famous in Marguerite Henry's book, *Misty of Chincoteague*. The legend has it that these island ponies are descendants of horses that swam ashore from a wrecked Spanish galleon centuries ago. The famous Wild Pony Roundup and Swim to Chincoteague is held annually in late July. It is a day of high spirits and good food.

In 1945, a launch site was established on Wallops Island by the Langley Research Center, then a field station of NASA. The site is on Route 13, the major north–south road to Chincoteague (Rt. 175 east to Chintoteague; Rt. 697 to Wallops). In the early years, research at

Wallops was concentrated on obtaining aerodynamic data at transonic and low supersonic speeds. Wallops has been the launch site of over 150 unmanned spacecrafts and today is used primarily to obtain scientific data about the atmosphere and space. It continues to be an active part of the NASA unmanned space program. Tours can be arranged, and it is possible to make reservations to watch the launching of minor satellites.

The string of barrier islands running the length of the peninsula remain a natural wilderness. They are inaccessible except by boat and are privately owned by the Nature Conservancy or the Government. Smith Island, the southernmost, was discovered by Capt. John Smith and named for himself. The Cape Charles lighthouse, the most powerful in Virginia, is on the island.

Tangier Island

Tangier Island in the heart of the Chesapeake can be visited by ferry from Reedville on Virginia's Northern Neck (US 360). The island was discovered by Capt. John Smith in 1608 and settlement was permanently established in 1686. There is no industry on the island and no cars are allowed. The population is only 800. The peace and quiet of the isolated village is a tonic after the hustle and bustle of the 20th Century. Transportation to the island is also possible via mail boat, leaving Crisfield, Maryland at noon each day (Rt. 413 from US 13).

PRACTICAL INFORMATION FOR VIRGINIA'S
EASTERN SHORE

PLACES TO STAY

MOTELS AND INNS. There aren't many motels or inns on this stretch of the peninsula, but neither are there many towns of any real size. This is part of the charm of Virginia's Eastern Shore. But then, of course, Norfolk isn't all that far to the south and Salisbury, Maryland is just up US 13 to the north.

Channel Bass Inn. *Expensive.* 100 Church Street, Chincoteague; 336–6148. Eleven rooms, many furnished with antiques, near the wildlife sanctuary.

America House. *Moderate.* On US 13 at the entrance to the Chesapeake Bay Bridge-Tunnel; 331–1776. 79 rooms with balconies, a private beach, sailboats, picnic tables, and grills.

The Driftwood Motor Lodge. *Moderate.* Beach Rd. at Assateague Bridge, Maddox Blvd. Chincoteague; 336–6557. 52 rooms with private patios and balconies overlooking the shore at the entrance to Assateague National Seashore.

Refuge Motor Inn. *Moderate.* One block west of Assateague Bridge Beach Rd., Chincoteague; 336–5511. 68 units with picnic tables and grills overlooking wildlife refuge. AE, MC, V.

Birchwood Motel. *Inexpensive.* 573 S. Main St., turn right when entering Chincoteague; 336–6133. 40 rooms.

Anchor Inn Motel. *Inexpensive to Moderate.* 534 S. Main St., Chincoteague, a quarter mile right after entering town; 336–6313. 12 rooms, with one efficiency. Located on Chicoteague Channel, near the boat harbor.

Island Motor Inn. *Moderate.* 711 N. Main St., Chincoteague; 336–3141. Waterfront rooms, some with balconies and boardwalk. Open all year. AE, MC, V.

Mariner Motel. *Inexpensive.* Maddox Blvd., Chincoteague; 336–6565. 88 rooms, 4 efficiencies. Pool.

Sea Shell Motel. *Inexpensive to Moderate.* 215 Willow St., a short block south on South Main, Chincoteague; 336–6589. 13 doubles, plus efficiencies. Pool.

PLACES TO EAT

Channel Bass. *Expensive.* 100 Church St., Chincoteague; 336–6148. Continental menu specializing in seafood español, backfin crab souffle, and oyster souffle. Elegant Colonial atmosphere. Chef-owned.

Misty. Maddox Blvd., Chincoteague; 336–3000. Specializes in steaks and seafood with a salad bar and wildlife decor.

Pony Pines. Church St. Extension, Chincoteague; 336–8964. Specializes in crab imperial and stuffed flounder. Chef-owned.

Hilda Crockett's Chesapeake House. *Inexpensive to Moderate.* On Main St., Tangier Island; 891–2240. Meals daily from April 15 through mid-October. Crab—cakes, fritters, however. Worth the ferry ride.

Amy Harold

NORFOLK AND VIRGINIA BEACH

by
EDGAR AND PATRICIA CHEATHAM

Norfolk

Site of the world's largest naval base and NATO's Atlantic head-quarters, this seafaring city now looks with pride to its waterfront. Stunning Waterside Festival Marketplace, designed by James Rouse Enterprises Development Corp. and boasting more than 100 boutiques, restaurants, lounges, and specialty shops, fronts on the Elizabeth River. So popular it is being doubled in size, Waterside has helped inspire the revitalization of downtown Norfolk. Neighboring Town Point Park is home each year to more than 230 free concerts and events and features ethnic foods, games, and live entertainment. Nearby, at Banana Pier, the prestigious Cousteau Society will soon open the Cousteau Oceans Center, a marine science research and exhibit complex headed by re-nowned explorer Jacques Cousteau.

In downtown Norfolk, historic Selden and Monticello Arcades have been handsomely restored, as has a jewel-like landmark hotel, The Madison. Ghent and The Hague, attractive in-town neighborhoods, have been refurbished and renovated into a pleasing mix of traditional and contemporary decor.

Norfolk's waterfront also includes Ocean View, bordering Chesa-peake Bay. This 14-mile stretch of sandy beaches and peaceful waters is ideal for family enjoyment. Ocean View is adjacent to the Norfolk end of the Bay Bridge-Tunnel.

Festivals have become a tradition in Norfolk. The April Internation-al Azalea Festival is followed by the May Ghent Arts Festival in Town Point Park, and the lavish three-day June Harborfest celebration with fireworks, tall ship parades, boat races, luscious seafoods, and live entertainment. In mid-October the Renaissance Faire livens the Water-side with music, dance, strolling minstrels, poetry, and Shakespeare readings.

Virginia Beach

Virginia Beach, one of the Eastern Seaboard's most popular and attractive seaside resorts, boasts 29 miles of fine sand beaches and offers superb surf swimming, waterskiing, boating, and fishing.

Atlantic Avenue, fronted by the city's famed boardwalk, has been revitalized and beautified as a pedestrian mall with greenery, benches, and public gathering spots. Free daily outdoor entertainment and Sun-day fireworks are offered Memorial Day through Labor Day. Also free "Summer Sundays on the Beach" concerts are held at the Norwegian Lady statue, 25th St. and Oceanfront, and family fun is the focus of "Saturdays at the Park" at various city parks.

Popular seasonal events include the late June Annual Boardwalk Art Show, Shakespeare-by-the-Sea Festival in late August at Pavilion Con-vention Center, and, the last weekend in September, the Virginia Beach Neptune Festival, with parades, dances, golf and tennis tournaments, arts and crafts, and seafood feasts. Throughout the summer, anglers can participate in a series of saltwater fishing tournaments for $15,000 in collective prize money.

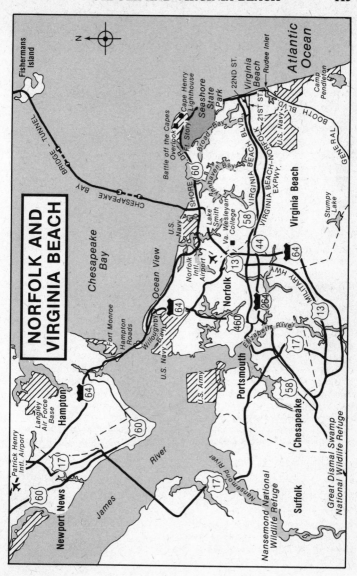

PRACTICAL INFORMATION
FOR NORFOLK AND VIRGINIA BEACH

PLACES TO STAY

HOTELS AND MOTELS. Most accommodations in Norfolk and Virginia Beach generally offer varied rate structures on a seasonal basis. Peak summer-season rates, particularly in the popular Virginia Beach resort area, are considerably lower at other times of the year. Here are general categories based on room rates per night, double occupancy: *Deluxe,* $100 and up; *Expensive,* $75 to $100; *Moderate,* $40 to $75; *Inexpensive,* below $40. Notations in the following listings indicate higher summer rates unless stated otherwise. Rates are subject to change without notice.

Norfolk

Hilton-Airport. *Expensive to Deluxe.* 1500 N. Military Highway at Northampton Blvd., 466–8000. Color TV, outdoor pool, tennis courts, health center with indoor pool, sauna, gym, Jacuzzi, lounge, specialty restaurant, coffee shop, nightclub.

Lagniappe. *Expensive to Deluxe.* 890 Poplar Hall Dr., 461–5956. All-suite hotel, color TV, outdoor pool, hot tub, steam room, complimentary breakfast, restaurant.

Omni International Hotel. *Expensive to Deluxe,* year-round rates. 777 Waterside Dr., 622–6664. Color TV, in-room movies, pool, valet parking, lounges, live entertainment, dancing, two restaurants, concierge, harborside location, convenient to Waterside Festival Marketplace.

Holiday Inn—Waterside Area, Downtown. *Expensive.* 700 Monticello Ave., 627–5555. Color TV with movie channel, Olympic size outdoor pool, racquetball, lounge, live entertainment, restaurant, shops, convenient to Scope Convention Center, free shuttle service to Waterside Festival Marketplace.

Hotel Madison. *Expensive to Deluxe.* Granby and Freemason Sts., 622–6682. Color TV, sauna, steambath, hot tub, in-room continental breakfast, valet parking, lounge, two restaurants, concierge; an elegantly restored traditional hostelry.

Ramada Inn Ocean View. *Moderate to Expensive.* 719 E. Ocean View Ave., 583–5211. Color TV, in-room movies, Olympic-size pool, beach across street, golf, tennis, lounge, entertainment, and restaurant.

Best Western Center Inn. *Moderate to Expensive,* year round rate. 1 Best Sq., 461–6600. Color TV, Olympic-size pool in courtyard, spa with indoor pool, sauna, Jacuzzi, lounge, and restaurant.

Econo Lodge. *Inexpensive to Moderate.* 1850 E. Little Creek Rd., 583–1561. Color TV, pool, nonsmokers' rooms, guest laundry, and lounges. Restaurants nearby.

Virginia Beach

Cavalier Hotel. *Expensive to Deluxe.* Atlantic Ave. and 42nd St., 425–8555. Cavalier Oceanfront is restored vintage hostelry dating from the early years of the century; the Oceanside Tower is contemporary. Color TV, outdoor and indoor pools, playgrounds, platform tennis, golf privileges, valet parking, laundry services, family restaurant, patio dining, and lounge. Supper club for dining and "Big Band" dancing; open year-round.

Crosswinds Resort Inn. *Expensive to Deluxe.* Atlantic Ave. and 11th St., 422–5000. Color TV, in-room movies, heated outdoor pool, laundry and dry cleaning services, golf, and off-season packages. Some suites with hot tubs and waterbeds. Restaurant, lounge, and Beach Cabaret nightclub with entertainment. Open year-round.

Hilton Inn. *Expensive to Deluxe.* Atlantic Ave. at 8th St., 428–8935. Color TV, heated indoor, outdoor, and kiddie pools, whirlpool, poolside cocktail and snack bars, marina, golf and tennis privileges, bridal rooms with mirrored ceilings, lounge with entertainment, and restaurant; open year-round.

Holiday Inn on the Ocean. *Expensive to Deluxe.* 3900 Atlantic Ave. at 39th St., 428–1711. Color TV, pool, lanai facing ocean, surfing, tennis, golf privileges, roof-top dining room, coffee shop, and lounge with entertainment; open year-round.

Holiday Inn Oceanfront Boardwalk. *Deluxe.* 2417 Atlantic Ave. at 25th St., 425–6920. Color TV, indoor pool, golf and tennis privileges, lounge with entertainment and restaurant; open year-round.

Howard Johnson's Motor Lodge. *Expensive.* 3705 Atlantic Ave. at 38th St., 428–7220. Color TV, in-room movies, oceanside pool, and coin laundry. Convenient to dinner theatres, shops, golf, fishing and tennis facilities. Lounge and restaurant; open year-round.

Princess Anne Inn. *Expensive to Deluxe.* Atlantic Ave. and 25th St. on the Ocean, 428–5611. Color TV, in-room movies, heated indoor pool with automated sunroof for tanning in any weather and giant sun solarium for natural tans, enclosed walkway from rooms to pool, whirlpool baths, dry sauna, oceanfront rooms with large glass-enclosed balconies, lounge, oceanside dining, and room service for all meals; open year-round.

Quality Inn Expressway. *Expensive.* 4564 Bonny Rd.; use Exit 3B from Rt. 44 to Independence Blvd., north ¼ mile to Bonny Rd., exit east to Inn, 497–4488. Color TV, in-room movies, outdoor pool, lounge, and restaurant; open year-round.

Ramada Inn Oceanside Tower. *Expensive.* Oceanfront at 57th St., 428–7025. Color TV, indoor-outdoor pool, health spa, atrium area, lounges, and restaurant; open year-round.

Sheraton Beach Inn & Conference Center. *Expensive to Deluxe.* Oceanfront at 36th St., 425–9000. Color TV, heated pool, laundry and dry cleaning service, golf, fishing and tennis nearby, recreation and game rooms, lounge with entertainment and dancing, and restaurants; open year-round.

Ocean House Motel. *Expensive to Deluxe.* Atlantic Ave. at 31st St., across the street from beach, 425–7730. Color TV, rooftop pool, Jacuzzi, sundeck, lounge, and restaurant; open year-round.

Pavilion Tower-A Dunfey Resort & Conference Center. *Expensive to Deluxe.* 1900 Pavilion Dr., adjacent to Virginia Beach Pavilion Convention Center, 228–2121. Color TV, in-room movies, indoor pool, all-weather tennis courts, health spa and fitness center, and complimentary transportation to the beach. Lounge and restaurant; open year-round.

Idlewhyle Motel & Efficiencies. *Moderate to Expensive.* Atlantic Ave. and 27th St., 428–9341. Color TV, in-room movies, outdoor heated pool, oceanfront location, baby-sitting service. Restaurant nearby; open year-round.

Bow Creek Motel. *Moderate.* 3429 Club House Rd., 340–1222. Color TV, pool, 18-hole public golf course adjacent. Lounge and restaurant; open year-round.

Econo Lodge *Inexpensive to Moderate.* On US 13, half-mile from junction with I-64, (5819 Northampton Blvd.), 464–9306. Color TV, in-room movies, some efficiencies available, and restaurant adjacent; open year-round.

 BED & BREAKFAST. For information about bed and breakfast choices in Norfolk, Virginia Beach, and vicinity, contact Ashby Willcox and Susan Hubbard, Bed & Breakfast of Tidewater Virginia, P.O. Box 3343, Norfolk, VA 23514, 627–1983 or 627–9409; call anytime, answering machine in use when coordinators are away from phone.

 CAMPGROUNDS. Virginia Beach campgrounds offer both seasonal and year-round facilities. Inquire about rates from individual establishments; pets on leash are accepted. Reservations advised, especially during peak summer vacation season. For further information, contact: Virginia Div. of Tourism, 202 N. Ninth St., Suite 500, Richmond, VA 23227; (804–786–4484). The following are available in the Virginia Beach area:

Best Holiday Trav-L-Park. 1075 General Booth Blvd.; Open year-round. Playground, 4 pools, 3 stores, LP gas, showers and restrooms, dumping station, water, electricity, sewer hookups, and tent sites, (425–0249).

KOA Campground. 1240 General Booth Blvd.; Open seasonally, inquire. Playground, 3 pools, store, LP gas, showers and restrooms, dumping station, water, electricity, sewer hookups, and tent sites, (428–1444).

North Bay Shore Campground. 3257 Colechester Rd., 23456; Open Apr.–Oct. Playground, pool, store, LP gas, showers and restrooms, dumping station, water and electricity, and tent sites, (426–7911).

Seashore State Park. 2500 Shore Dr., 23451. Open Apr.–Nov. Store, showers, and restrooms. Dumping station, but no water or electric hookups. Cabins available, additional fee for pets; reservations through Virginia State Parks or Ticketron, (490–3939.) Mon.–Fri., 10–4.

Seneca Campground. 144 S. Princess Anne Rd., 23457. Open year-round. Playground, pool, store, showers and restrooms, dumping station, and water and electricity hookups, (426–6241).

Surfside at Sandbridge. 3665 Sandpiper Rd., 23456. Open Mar.–Nov. Playground, store, showers and restrooms, dumping station, and water and electricity sites, (426–2911).

PLACES TO EAT

RESTAURANTS. Fresh Chesapeake Bay seafood is the order of the day in many popular Norfolk and Virginia Beach restaurants, but steak lovers will find many seafood establishments cater to their strange tastes as well. Ask about Early Bird, daily specials, and child's plates. Those listed accept at least two major credit cards (MC, V). Estimated costs are per person excluding wine, cocktails, and tips. *Deluxe:* $25 or more, *Expensive:* $15–$25; *Moderate:* $7–$15; *Inexpensive:* under $7.

Norfolk

Le Charlieu. *Expensive.* 112 College Pl., 623–7202. Intimate dining with a French touch, in restored Downtown area. Lunch and dinner. Reservations. Coat and tie requested.

Embassy Room. *Expensive.* The Madison Hotel, Granby & Freemason Sts., 622–6682. Veal Oscar and fresh seafoods are specialties in this elegantly traditional dining room.

Esplanade. *Expensive.* Omni International Hotel, 777 Waterside Dr., 623–0333. Elegant small gourmet dining room offers impeccable service and superb American and Continental cuisine. Dinner only, Mon.–Sat. Reservations. Jacket and tie requested.

Lockhart's of Norfolk. *Moderate to Expensive.* 8440 Tidewater Dr., 588–0405. One of area's oldest and most popular restaurants for seafood and prime ribs. Nautical decor, with antiques. Family proprietors grow their own vegetables.

Ship's Cabin Seafood Restaurant. *Moderate to Expensive.* 4110 E. Ocean View Ave., 583–4659. This very popular award-winning seafood restaurant serves mesquite-grilled fresh fish and choice steaks. Good choice of Virginia and California wines. Dinner only.

Il Porto of Norfolk. *Moderate.* 333 Waterside Dr., 627–4400. Taverna setting, Italian specialties; overlooks harbor. Evening ragtime piano.

Szechuan Garden Chinese Restaurant. *Inexpensive to Moderate.* 123 W. Charlotte St., 627–6130. Authentic Szechuan cuisine; friendly, personalized service; locally popular. Lunch and dinner. Reservations requested.

Virginia Beach

Orion's Roof. *Expensive to Deluxe.* Top of the Cavalier, Atlantic Ave. at 42nd St., 425–8555. Continental menu, live entertainment, and dancing in a sophisticated supper club.

Blue Pete's. *Moderate to Expensive.* 1400 N. Muddy Creek Rd., 426–2278. Casual seafood restaurant, locally popular. Noted for sweet-potato biscuits and fresh vegetables. Outdoor lounge, live entertainment.

The Lighthouse. *Moderate to Expensive.* Rudee Inlet at 1st St. & Atlantic Ave., 428–9851 or 428–7974. Maine lobster and Eastern Shore seafoods, with its own bakery. Sunday brunch.

Poppie's. *Moderate to Expensive.* Pavilion Tower/Dunfey Resort & Conference Center, 1900 Pavilion Dr., 422–8900. Choice specialties in multi-level restaurant.

That Seafood Place. *Moderate to Expensive.* Holiday Inn-on-the-Ocean, 39th & Atlantic Ave., 428–1711 or 428–2411. Skytop restaurant and lounge. Seafoods, steaks, and lavish salad bar.

Wesley's. *Moderate to Expensive.* 32nd St. & Holly Rd., 422–1511. Creole-accented steaks, and seafood; menu changes weekly. Peanut butter cheese cake a specialty. Extensive wine cellar.

Ocean Crab House. *Moderate.* 15th St. & Oceanfront, 428–6186. Seafood buffet, à la carte service. Home baked desserts.

Sir Richard's. *Inexpensive to Moderate.* 21st St. & Atlantic Ave., 428–1926. Prime rib, steaks, and seafoods; daily specials. Live entertainment.

Caesar's Restaurant. *Inexpensive.* 2312 Atlantic Ave., 422–3232. Veal, seafood, Italian cuisine. Early Bird specials. Live entertainment. Extensive wine list. Local following.

Mary's Kountry Kitchen. *Inexpensive.* 17th St., 5 blocks from Oceanfront, 428–9805. Home-cooked breakfast, lunch, dinner.

THINGS TO SEE AND DO

Norfolk

GARDENS. Norfolk Botanical Gardens. Located on Airport Rd., Norfolk's 175-acre botanical gardens are site of International Azalea Festival and one of nation's top Rose Display Gardens. Open daily. Seasonal boat, mini-train tours, picnicking, restaurant, and gift shop.

HISTORIC SITES. Moses Myers House, 323 E. Freemason St., classic Georgian structure; **St. Paul's Episcopal Church,** 201 St. Paul's Blvd., sole survivor of British bombardment of 1776, with a cannonball still embedded in one wall; **Willoughby-Baylor House,** 601 E. Freemason St., fine period furnishings, and charming herb and flower garden. All closed Mon., some holidays.

MUSEUMS. Chrysler Museum. Olney Rd. and Mowbray Arch. Among the nation's top 20 museums. Notable for its ancient collections, and major European and American art. Decorative Arts collection and home of Chrysler Institute of Glass. This major collection includes Tiffany and Sandwich glass. Closed Mon., major holidays. Branch at Seaboard Center, 235 E. Plume St., offers several exhibits for Downtown visitors, Mon.–Fri.

The Hermitage Foundation Museum. 7637 North Shore Rd. English Tudor mansion on garden grounds fronting Lafayette River. Displays rare Oriental and Western art treasures. 10–5 Mon.–Sat., 1–5 Sun. Closed major holidays.

Douglas MacArthur Memorial. Plume and Bank Sts. in historic 1850 City Hall. The final resting place of General MacArthur. Extensive exhibits and film, chronicling his life. Open daily. Free.

NATIONAL PARKS. Dismal Swamp National Wildlife Refuge. Located approximately 24 miles southwest of Norfolk, via I-64 and US 17 S., is rare geographic area of peat bogs and thick forest, laced by manmade canals. Refuge for migratory birds, waterfowl, and black bears, Dismal Swamp was surveyed by George Washington in 1763. In its center is Lake Drummond, which can be explored by boat tours along the Dismal Swamp Canal.

ZOOS. Lafayette Zoological Park. 3500 Granby St. on 55 wooded acres beside the Lafayette River. The zoo houses animals in natural habitat environments. Children's petting zoo. Open daily except major holidays.

SPECIAL INTEREST. Norfolk Naval Station. 9809 Hampton Blvd. The Naval Station is home port for more than 123 ships and aircraft squadrons, plus shore-based military activities. Tours of ships every weekend, year-round; base tours Mar.–Nov.

LIVELY ARTS. Norfolk is witnessing a cultural "boom." **Virginia Opera Assoc.,** one of nation's top regional companies, performs at Center Theater; **Virginia Symphony Orchestra** appears at Chrysler Hall, Scope Cultural and Convention Center; **Feldman String Quartet** offers seasonal performances in Chrysler Museum Theater; the **Virginia Stage Company** performs at historic **Wells Theater; Riverview Playhouse,** community theater of Old Dominion University, presents classical, traditional, avant-garde fare; **Tidewater Dinner Theatre,** grounds of Lake Wright Resort Complex, 6270 Northampton Blvd., offers buffet dinner professional theater, Wed.–Sat.; and **Little Theatre of Norfolk** is one of nation's oldest amateur groups.

WATER SPORTS. Charter Fishing, Chesapeake Bay Fishing, Charter Yacht Kittiwake, 3512 Dominion Ave.; Cobbs Marina, 4524 Dunning Rd.; **Fishing Piers,** Harrison Boathouse & Pier, 414 W. Ocean View Ave.; Ocean View Fishing Pier, 300 E. Ocean View Ave.; Sea Gull Fishing Pier, Chesapeake Bay Bridge-Tunnel; and Willoughby Bay Marina, 1651 Bayville St.; **Fresh Water Fishing**—Lakes Prince and Smith; rental boats and launching ramps.

SAILING. Charters, Rover Marine Inc., 1651 Bayville St.; lessons, Kitty Hawk Sports, Inc., 333 Waterside Dr., Apr.–Oct.

SPECTATOR SPORTS. Norfolk's Met Park is scene of minor league play between the Tidewater Tides (New York Mets affiliate) and other AAA teams.

STATE PARKS. *False Cape,* accessible only by a 5-mile walk, bicycle ride, or a boat trip through Back Bay Wildlife Refuge, has maritime forests and natural dunes along the Atlantic Shore. *Seashore,* located at Cape Henry on US 60, has visitor center, guided walks, and biking over 27 miles of nature trails. The first English colonists to the Chesapeake landed on Cape Henry in 1607.

TOURING INFORMATION. Most of Norfolk's attractions are located on or near the water. This is a seaport town that has rediscovered its nautical heritage. The tours below reflect a renewed interest in Norfolk's magnificent harbor

By Auto: Follow Norfolk Tour signs to attractions.

By Bicycle: Rentals from The Waterside "Ask Me" kiosk, May–Sept.

By Boat: Various seasonal excursions aboard *Carrie B* riverboat replica; *New Spirit* launch; *American Rover* topsail schooner; *Bonny Jean Rover* sailing yacht; *Dixie Rover* paddle wheeler; *Norfolk Rover* topsail schooner.

By Bus: Tours of world's largest naval base Mar.–Nov. Tickets, departure at The Waterside, Naval Base Tour Office.

By Guided Tour: for list of companies, also complete sightseeing information, contact Norfolk Convention & Visitors Bureau, Monticello Arcade, Norfolk, VA 23510, 441-5266. Or drop by Bureau Visitor Centers: Ocean View, W. End of 4th St., off I-64, 588-0404, or The Waterside, second level, "Ask Me" booth, 622-0990.

Virginia Beach

Virginia Beach's free Boardwalk runs three and a half miles along the resort's magnificent broad and sandy beach, from Rudee Inlet at 2nd St. northward to

38th St. The area is covered by lifeguards; and rental folding chairs, floats, and beach umbrellas are available.

HISTORIC SITES. DeWitt Cottage (1895). The Cottage, which reflects early beach life, can be viewed from Boardwalk at 11th St.; **First Landing Cross (Cape Henry Memorial),** within Fort Story Military Reservation, marks the spot where Jamestown colonists first touched New World shores on April 26, 1607; **Old Cape Henry Lighthouse** (1791) is adjacent to the entrance to Chesapeake Bay; **Lynnhaven House** (ca. 1680), reflects fine masonry and decorative arts, open Apr.–Nov., Tues.–Sun., 12–4; **Adam Thoroughgood House** (1636), is believed to be the nation's oldest brick home, open 10–5, Tues.–Sat. Apr.–Nov., 12–5 Dec.–Mar., closed holidays; **Princess Anne Courthouse** (1824), 9 miles southwest via Rts. 615 and 149, in Princess Anne, stands beside the impressive and beautifully landscaped **Municipal Center,** open 9–5 Mon.–Fri.

MUSEUMS. Virginia Beach Arts Center, 18th and Arctic Ave., with changing exhibits, moves in 1986 to site across from the Pavilion, off Rte. 44, Virginia Beach Expressway; **Virginia Beach Maritime Historical Museum,** 24th & Oceanfront, in 1903 Seatack Lifesaving Station, houses ship models, artifacts, and shipwreck mememtos; open daily Memorial Day–Oct., closed Mon. rest of year; **Virginia Museum of Marine Sciences,** 717 General Booth Blvd., has unique hands-on marine exhibits, finny habitats, and a 100,000-gallon aquarium. The museum offers simulated deep ocean dives; and **Royal London Wax Museum,** 1606 Atlantic Ave., with over 100 life-size figures in realistic settings. Open year-round.

SPECIAL INTEREST. Association for Research and Enlightenment, Inc. *(ARE),* 67th & Atlantic, ESP exploration center, offers free daily lectures, films, and tours, based on works of Edgar Cayce, history's best-documented psychic; **Little Creek Amphibious Base** (passes at Main Gate, Shore Dr.) welcomes visitors to museum and weekend ship open houses: **Norwegian Lady,** 9-foot bronze statue at 25th & Oceanfront commemorates 1891 sinking of Norwegian ship *Diktator,* a gift from sister city of Moss, Norway; **Oceana Naval Air Station,** Oceana Blvd., offers take-off and landing views of advanced Navy aircrafts; and **Wildwater Rapids,** General Booth Blvd., a family oriented water park that features splashy slides, wave pools, and innertube rides.

LIVELY ARTS. The **Virginia Symphony Orchestra** presents four annual concerts at Pavilion Theater, which is also site of the *Virginia Symphony Pops* series, performances by **Tidewater Ballet Association.**

SPORTS. The emphasis, of course, is on the water and water-related activities, but Virginia Beach also has a full measure of fun-in-the-sun participant sports.

Boating Ramps: free at Owl Creek, General Booth Blvd.; Munden Point Park, Munden Point Rd.

Charter Boat Deep Sea Fishing; Bubba's Marina, 3323 Shore Dr.; D&M Marina, 3311 Shore Dr.; Virginia Beach Fishing Center, 200 Winston-Salem Ave.

Fishing Piers: Little Island, Sandbridge, Atlantic Ocean; Lynnhaven Inlet, Starfish Rd., Chesapeake Bay; Rudee Inlet Fishing Site, south end; Sea Gull, Chesapeake Bay Bridge-Tunnel; Virginia Beach, 15th St. & Oceanfront.

Golfing: on six championship courses—challenging new Hell's Point, Red Wing, Bow Creek, Stumpy Lake, Kempsville Meadows, Lake Wright.

Scuba, Snorkeling: lessons, gear, trips from Lynnhaven Dive Center, 1413 Great Neck Rd.; Scuba Ventures, 2247-B N. Great Neck Rd.

Tennis: on 156 courts, most lighted, including Owl Creek Municipal Tennis Center, considered one of nation's 50 best such complexes.

SHOPPING. Virginia Beach has become one of the nation's fastest-growing centers for off-price shopping, with well over 125 stores discounting designer fashions and name-brand items. Major centers within a 15-minute drive of the oceanfront include *Great American Outlet Mall; Lynnhaven Mall,* with 140 stores including six major department stores; *Pembroke Mall; Military Circle;* and *Pacific Place* with quality designer wear, collector and decorative art works, jewelry, china, crafts. The *Virginia Beach Maritime Historical Museum* (see above) has an outstanding gift shop featuring nautical items, clocks, brasses, prints, and jewelry.

TOURING INFORMATION. Virginia Beach is an ocean resort and most of its touring attractions are located at or near the surf and the Boardwalk.

By Auto: Self-guided tour follows prominent road signs to major landmarks and attractions (see address and phone below).

By Bicycle: Rentals available along the Boardwalk for following oceanfront trail.

By Trolley: Tidewater Regional Transit Authority (TRT) vehicles run mid-May–summer from Rudee Inlet to 42nd St., and Redwing Park to the Civic Center (The Dome). Shuttles also run to Lynnhaven and Pembroke Malls and there's service to Norfolk and back via the Oceanside/Waterside Express, which runs between The Dome and Waterside. TRT also offers tours to Norfolk Naval Station, downtown Norfolk.

By Boat: Cruises aboard *Miss Virginia Beach* from Virginia Beach Fishing Center.

For sightseeing information: Virginia Beach Visitors Information Center, 19th St. & Pacific Ave., Virginia Beach, VA 23451, 425–7511. The Center provides a free continuous audiovisual presentation about the beach and the resort's attractions.

TIDEWATER VIRGINIA

by
RODNEY N. SMITH

Tidewater Virginia is the oldest part of America, a romantic land of elegant plantations and horse-drawn carriages, historic churches, and famous battlefields. It is a place of unspoiled beaches, Colonial taverns, and some of the finest nautical and space museums in the country.

In the beginning there was only Jamestown. In 1607 America's first permanent but struggling English settlement was established on Jamestown Island. The "feel" of Jamestown is recaptured today in the Old Church Tower and reconstructed church and the early foundations and unearthed streets of this first settlement. At nearby Jamestown Festival Park there are full-scale replicas of James Fort and the three tiny ships that brought those first English settlers to the shores of the New World —*Susan Constant, Godspeed,* and *Discovery.*

Tidewater Virginia is also the home of Colonial Williamsburg, the largest restored 18th Century town in America. Here visitors will find charming old taverns and Colonial homes and stately public buildings such as the Colonial Capitol and the 17th Century Wren Building on the campus of the College of William and Mary. Between the College and Colonial Williamsburg, up and down the length of Duke of Gloucester Street, every by-way thrills and delights us. A fife and drum corps marches past, a beautiful garden comes into view, or an expert artisan demonstrates his skill, producing a barrel or a basket or a candle or a silver bowl. Many of these hand-made "Colonial" wares can be bought in the charming shops about the village.

From Williamsburg, the beautiful Colonial National Parkway leads the visitor to Yorktown, where the Revolutionary War ended and a new nation had won its right to be born. Visitors should see the Yorktown Victory Center and National Park Visitors' Center, the picturesque village, and the famous battlefield. They should also try the little seafood restaurants beside the Bay, for Yorktown is home to some of America's finest fresh seafood.

Tidewater Plantations

Amid the landmarks and monuments northwest of Norfolk, nothing better recaptures early American antebellum life than the majestic plantations along the James. Tidewater Virginia has been amply blessed with some magnificent survivors. These marvelous mansions flourished along the James River from Williamsburg to Richmond and throughout the Tidewater and Northern Neck regions. Their legends are a delight. The Rolfe–Warren House stands on land given to John Rolfe by his father-in-law, Chief Powhatan. Other plantations are the ancestral or actual homes of Presidents. George Washington was born here on the banks of Pope's Creek, and Berkely Plantation is said—by Virginians—to have been the site of America's first Thanksgiving in 1619, a year before the Pilgrims *landed* at Plymouth Rock.

Tidewater Virginia is the oldest part of the state, but it also glitters brightest. Visitors can find lively golden beaches, such as world-famous Virginia Beach (see previous chapter). Popular for its sun, surf, and seafood, Virginia Beach is celebrated as one of the country's outstanding ocean resorts for fun-filled family vacations, while its neighbor, Norfolk, has rediscovered itself and its magnificent harbor.

On the Harbor

Nearby are the harbor towns, with attractions as varied as Portsmouth's Naval Shipyard Museum; Norfolk's Chrysler Museum and

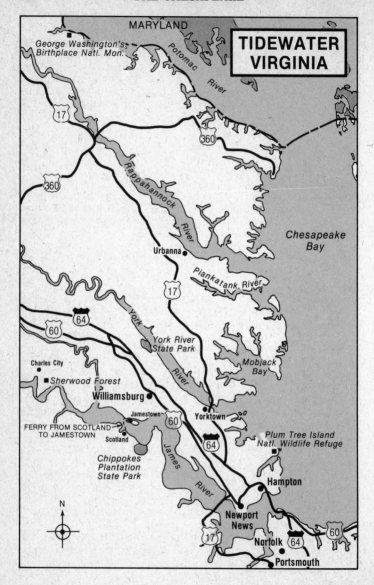

Scope Convention and Cultural Center; and Hampton's old St. John's Church, historic Fort Monroe, and the Hampton Coliseum.

And here too is family fun at Busch Garden's *The Old Country,* which has thrilling rides and shows, shops, and stirring oompah bands —and has something for every age.

A Tidewater vacation in the Chesapeake Vacationland can range between a visit to one of the best theme parks in the world to a day in the sun on a wide stretch of golden sand, or from the pleasures of the moment to an appreciation of the past.

EXPLORING WILLIAMSBURG

Colonial Williamsburg is the site of one of the most extensive restorations ever undertaken. Visitors experience life as it was lived in George Washington's day in this small Colonial village. History lives in Williamsburg's functioning shops, its craftspeople at work at their specialties, and in authentic taverns serving food and drink that would have been offered in the 18th Century when this town was the capital of English Virginia.

The 173-acre Historic Area is centered around Duke of Gloucester Street, which runs about one mile from the College of William and Mary, where Thomas Jefferson studied, to the Capitol, where Patrick Henry denounced King George III's stamp tax. The streets are lined with old homes, taverns, stores, and craft shops.

In addition to the buildings open to the public and the shops, visitors can enjoy dining in one of the village's authentic Colonial taverns. The rich variety of food offered in the 18th Century has been carefully recreated, and is also available in the many restaurants located in and around this historic area. Shopping is another aspect of a Williamsburg visit, and tempting souvenirs of your trip abound in craft shops, gift shops, and stores in the Virginia Peninsula.

All this is part of the Colonial experience in Williamsburg, where three centuries ago the town was capital of England's largest colony in America. As such, Williamsburg played a vital role in the struggle for freedom and the representative government we now enjoy.

Williamsburg became the second capital of Virginia in 1699. It replaced Jamestown, the first permanent English settlement in the New World, where colonists had battled Indians, fire, famine, and pestilence since 1607. The Virginia Assembly selected Middle Plantation for the new capital and renamed it Williamsburg in honor of their English king.

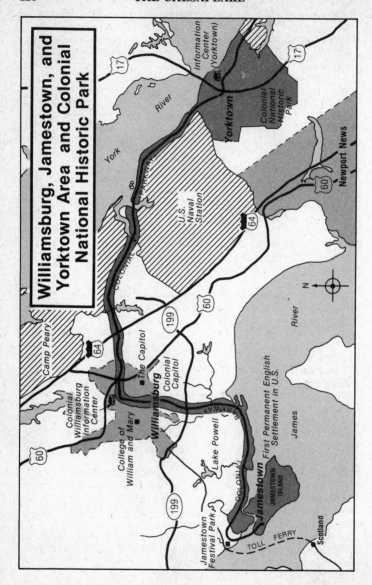

Williamsburg, Jamestown, and Yorktown Area and Colonial National Historic Park

The new city was already the site of the second college in America. Six years before, in 1693, a royal charter had been granted for an institution that would be named in honor of the British sovereigns, King William and Queen Mary. The royal governor and the Assembly carefully set about raising a new and well-ordered capital, one of the first planned cities in America.

An old horseway running the length of the settlement was straightened, widened, and renamed Duke of Gloucester Street. At the east end, facing the handsome Wren Building a mile away, the first government building in America to be given the dignified name of Capitol was built. Midway between the College and the Capitol, a residence for the royal governor was completed in 1720. Known as the Governor's Palace, it was in time occupied by seven royal governors and the first two governors of the Commonwealth of Virginia, Patrick Henry and Thomas Jefferson (who moved the capital to Richmond in 1780 because of the threat of a British attack).

Many weathered landmarks survived to the 20th Century. The Rev. W.A.R. Goodwin, then rector of Bruton Parish Church, recognized the significance of these remaining structures. Through the minister's efforts and enthusiasm, John D. Rockefeller, Jr. became interested and in 1926 the first steps were taken to preserve and restore the city's Historic Area.

The two men began a modest project to preserve a few of the more important buildings but, as the work progressed, it also expanded to include the major portion of the Colonial capital. Today, approximately 85 percent of 18th Century Williamsburg is encompassed by the undertaking. Rockefeller gave the project his personal leadership until his death in 1960, and it was his generosity and uncompromising ethic of excellence that guided and dominated its development. The old city today appears much as it did when Patrick Henry thundered his defiance of King George ii, and Virginia burgesses voted their historic resolution for independence.

Carter's Grove

Nearby Carter's Grove Plantation, located seven miles from Williamsburg on the banks of the James River, has a mansion that has been called "the most beautiful house in America." Carter's Grove was the breadbasket of Williamsburg in Colonial times. One of the great plantation homes of Colonial Virginia, Carter's Grove stands majestically on 600 acres of rolling countryside. Stretching 200 feet from end to end, this Georgian mansion was completed in the 1750s. It was renovated in 1929 by Mr. and Mrs. Archibald McCrea.

Remains of the 17th Century Wolstenholme Towne have also been discovered by Williamsburg archaeologists. Aided by archaeological investigations, the development of the gardens and the disclosure of Wolstenholme Towne are on-going projects that should in time enhance our understanding and appreciation of Colonial America.

Busch Gardens

Not everything about a Williamsburg visit is tied to our Colonial past; Busch Gardens, a modern theme park in 360 acres of beautiful Virginia forest, is only a few miles away. Its theme *The Old Country,* is presented in sections that recreate the romance, atmosphere, and architectural highlights of the British Isles, France, Germany, and Italy. Keyed to the four themes are live entertainment, shops, and restaurants. Among the most thrilling rides at Busch Gardens is the sensational Loch Ness Monster. Some of the biggest and brightest stars of today's entertainment world appear at Busch Gardens on special dates.

PRACTICAL INFORMATION
FOR IN AND AROUND WILLIAMSBURG

PLACES TO STAY

HOTELS AND MOTELS. There is no shortage of good accommodations in the Williamsburg-Busch Gardens area, but you may not believe that if you neglect to book well ahead during the peak summer touring season. Although space limitations restrict the length of the following list, we have attempted to provide a representative *selection,* keeping convenience, personal tastes, and the traveler's pocketbook always in mind. In general, but *only* in general, our categories follow the same price ranges that appear elsewhere in this guide: *Deluxe,* $100 and up; *Expensive,* $75 to $100; *Moderate,* $40 to $75, and *Inexpensive,* under $40. All are based on double occupancy.

Williamsburg Inn. *Deluxe.* S. Francis St., Colonial Williamsburg; 229–1000; res. (800) 446–8956. 232 rooms in the Inn and the Colonial houses, some more than 200 years old. All in the Historic Area. The Inn is elegantly furnished in regency style; the houses are restored buildings with 18th Century decor. Restaurant, golf, and tennis. AE, MC, V.

Williamsburg Hospitality House. *Expensive.* 415 Richmond Rd., 2 blocks west of the Inn; 229–4020 or (800) 446–9204. 315 rooms near the Historic Area. Golf privileges. AE, CB, DC, MC, V.

Williamsburg Lodge. *Expensive.* S. England St., near the Inn; 229–1000 or (800) 446–8956. 198 rooms at the edge of the Historic Area. Beautiful gardens. Restaurant. AE, CB, DC, MC, V.

Holiday Inn-East. *Moderate.* 804 Capitol Landing Rd., a short drive east on Rt. 5; 229–0200. 136 rooms near the Visitors Center. Restaurant. Major credit cards.

Ramada Inn-East. *Moderate.* 351 York St., 2 blocks east on US 60E. 201 rooms in a convenient location. Restaurant and pool. Major credit cards.

Sheraton Patriot Inn. *Moderate.* 3032 Richmond Rd., 3 miles west on US 60; 565–2600. 160 rooms. Restaurant, pool. AE, DC, CB, MC, V.

Fort Magruder Inn & Conference Center. *Moderate.* 6945 Pocahontas Trail; 220–2250. 304 rooms with local entertainment, lighted tennis, and golf privileges. Some rooms with private patios and balconies and some outside dining. AE, CB, DC, MC, V.

Best Western Patrick Henry Inn. *Inexpensive to Moderate.* York and Page Sts., Rt. 60E, 2 blocks east of the Colonial Capitol; 229–9540. 262 rooms. Convenient location and golf privileges. Restaurant. Major credit cards.

Best Western Williamsburg. *Moderate.* R. 60E at Rt. 199 overpass, a mile from Busch Gardens and just under 2 miles from Williamsburg; 446–9288. 135 rooms. Pool with sundeck. Restaurant. Major credit cards.

Greenbrier Lodge. *Inexpensive to Moderate.* 800 Capitol Landing Rd.; 229–2374 or (800) 368–2374. 57 rooms in a resort location. Restaurant and pool. AE, CB, DC, MC, V.

George Washington Inn. *Inexpensive.* 500 Merrimac Trail, a mile and a half east on Rt. 143; 229–7564. 140 rooms. Some credit cards.

Governor Spottswood Motel. *Inexpensive.* 1508 Richmond Rd., northwest about 2 miles on US 60W; 229–6444. 74 rooms. Picnic tables on a shaded lawn. Some credit cards.

Holiday Inn-West. *Inexpensive to Moderate.* 902 Richmond Rd.; 229–5060. 100 rooms with golf privileges. Downtown location. Restaurant. Major credit cards.

John Rolfe Motel. *Inexpensive.* 1313 N. Mount Vernon Ave., three-quarters of a mile from Williamsburg off Richmond Rd.; 220–1710. 28 rooms with kitchen units available. Pool.

King William Inn. *Inexpensive to Moderate.* 824 Capitol Landing Rd., a half mile northeast on Rt. 5; 229–4933 or (800) 446–1041. 183 rooms, some with balconies.

Minuet Manor. *Inexpensive to Moderate.* 1408 Richmond Road, slightly more than a mile northwest on US 60W; 220–2367. 112 rooms with tennis. Restaurant. AE, MC, V.

The Motor House. *Moderate.* One mile southeast of I-64, opposite the Information Center; 229–1000 or (800) 582–8976. 164 rooms with golf and tennis plans. Tennis and golf privileges, putting green, lawn games, and miniature golf. AE, MC, V.

Quality Inn–Colony. *Moderate.* 909 Page St., at junction of US 60E and VA 162; 229–1855. 59 rooms. Restaurant and pool. Major credit cards.

Quality Inn–Lord Paget. *Moderate.* 901 Capitol Landing Rd., a mile and a half east on Rt. 5; 229–4444. 88 rooms on a resort location with a small lake. All major credit cards.

Quality Inn–Mount Vernon. *Inexpensive to Moderate.* 1600 Richmond Rd., 2 miles northwest on US 60; 229–2401. 65 rooms on spacious grounds. AE, CB, DC, MC, V.

Sheraton Governor's Inn. *Moderate.* 506 N. Henry St., three and a half blocks north on Rt. 132; 229–6605. 72 rooms. Golf privileges. Pool. Major credit cards.

Hilton Inn Williamsburg. *Expensive.* 50 Kingsmill Dr., two and a half miles east on US 60, I-64 exit Busch Gardens; 220–2500. 300 rooms with Williamsburg and Busch Gardens plans. Some units with private patios and balconies. Restaurants, bar, room service, and pool. All major credit cards.

Econo Lodge–Williamsburg. *Inexpensive.* 505 York St., Rt. 60 east; 220–3100. 100 rooms. Pool. Morning coffee.

Econo Lodge–Restored Area. *Inexpensive.* 442 Parkway Dr. and Capitol Landing Rd., Exit 56 off I-64; 229–7564. 48 rooms. Restaurant adjacent.

Ironbound Inn. *Inexpensive.* 1220 Richmond Rd., 7 blocks west; 229–1532. 21 rooms. Pool. Free morning coffee. Most credit cards.

Motel 6. *Inexpensive.* 3030 Richmond Rd., two and a half miles northwest on US 60W; 565–2710. 169 rooms. Pool. Restaurant nearby. MC, V.

Quarterpath Inn. *Inexpensive.* 620 York St., a mile and a half east on US 60E; 220–0960 or (800) 446–9222. 90 rooms. Restaurant nearby. Pool. AE, CB, DC, MC, V.

PLACES TO EAT

RESTAURANTS. Dining in and around Williamsburg should be a joy, hopefully never traumatic. As is true in any major touring center, restaurants—even the most expensive—tend to be crowded during the summer touring season and we do strongly recommend that you make reservations if at all possible. The following selection of restaurants is not meant to be all-inclusive; there are simply too many fine places to eat in the Colonial National Historical Park area. We've tried to tailor this list of *selections* to a variety of tastes and pocketbooks, but if you discover "a very special place" that we've neglected or overlooked, we'd be delighted to hear about it.

Regency Room–Williamsburg Inn. *Expensive.* Francis St., Historic Area; 229–2141. Fine dining in an elegant setting. Continental menu. Specialties include rack of lamb and veal with morrel sauce. AE, MC, V.

Josiah Chowning's Tavern. *Expensive.* Duke of Gloucester St. at Queen St.; 229–2141. One of the authentic Colonial taverns of Williamsburg, featuring genuine fare such as Brunswick stew and Welsh rabbit in beer. Alehouse atmosphere. AE, MC, V.

Christiana Campbell's Tavern. *Expensive.* Waller St., across the lawn from the Colonial Capitol; 229–2141. Another of the three Colonial taverns happily still in operation. Specialties include spoon bread, seafood jambalaya, and fruit sherbet. George Washington ate here often, but in the private rooms. AE, MC, V.

King's Arms Tavern. *Expensive.* Duke of Gloucester St.; 229–2141. The most genteel of the 18th Century taverns. Specialties include Colonial game pies, scalloped oyster, and Sally Lunn bread. Colonial decor. AE, MC, V.

Kingsmill. *Expensive.* 100 Golf Club Rd., two and a half miles east of US 60E exit off I-64, Busch Gardens; 253–3900. Continental menu featuring escalope de veau, duck, and fresh seafood. Contemporary decor. Some credit cards.

Layfayette. *Expensive.* 1203 Richmond Rd.; 229–3811. Continental fare specializing in rack of lamb, shrimp, and lobster. Reservations recommended. Some credit cards.

Le Yaca. *Expensive.* 915 Pocohantas Trail in the Kingsmill Shops, US 60E; 220–3616. French cookery with a good wine cellar. Open-spit rack of lamb and Le Yaca's own special pastries. An elegant dining room. All major credit cards.

Trellis. *Expensive.* Duke of Gloucester St., Merchant's Square in the Historic Area; 229–8610. Continental menu. Specialties include fresh seafood and mesquite grilling. Homemade ice cream and pasta. Dinner reservations suggested. Some credit cards.

Williamsburg Lodge. *Expensive.* S. England St.; 229–1600. Offers a Chesapeake buffet Fridays and Saturdays. A pleasant garden cocktail lounge. Most credit cards.

Cascades at Motor House Motel. *Moderate.* Opposite Information Ctr.; 229–1000. Specializes in seafood and beef. AE, MC, V.

Whaling Company. *Moderate.* 494 McLaw Circle; 229–8610. Continental menu specializing in mesquite grilling and fresh seafood. AE, MC, V.

Aberdeen Barn. *Inexpensive to Moderate.* 1601 Richmond Rd.; 229–6661. Relaxed atmosphere with an open-hearth grill. Specializes in roast prime ribs, steak, and seafood. Some credit cards.

Lobster House. *Inexpensive to Moderate.* 1425 Richmond Rd.; 229–7771. Lobster is a specialty. Also other seafood and steak. Salty atmosphere. Most major credit cards.

THINGS TO SEE AND DO

There is a lot to see and do in Williamsburg. Not all of it is in the Historic Area, but that is where most visitors start. Visitors to Colonial Williamsburg should stop first at the Visitors Center, where they can buy tickets and get sightseeing information. The Center can also help with food and lodging reservations and suggestions. There is a cafeteria and a bookstore at the Center, as well as an orientation film presentation. This is where the free buses start that take visitors around the extensive restored site.

HISTORIC AREA. The Capitol at the east end of Duke of Gloucester Street is probably the most important building in the Historic Area. The General Assembly met here from 1704 to 1709 and it was here that Patrick Henry delivered his famous "Give me liberty or give me death" speech against the Stamp Act.

The Public Gaol is north of the Capitol across Nicholson St. This is where debtors, pirates (including Blackbeard's crew), and criminals were jailed.

A few steps west and back on Duke of Gloucester Street is Raleigh Tavern. The Tavern was a frequent meeting place for Washington, Jefferson, Henry, and other Revolutionary partriots and was for a time the social center of the Virginia Colony. It is open to the public, but no longer offers food or lodging. Wetherburn's Tavern, one of the most popular of the period, is directly across the street.

The Governor's Palace and gardens at the north end of the Palace Green was the home of seven royal governors and Virginia's first two governors, Henry and Jefferson. One of the most elegant buildings in Colonial America, it is set in 10 acres of beautifully restored formal gardens.

Just southeast of the Palace is Brush–Everard House, the home of one of the early mayors. It has a hand-carved staircase and beautiful boxwood gardens. The Peyton Randolph House (1716) is just to its southeast. This was the home of the President of the First Continental Congress and headquarters of General Rochambeau prior to the Battle of Yorktown.

Southwest of that is the James Geddy House, once the home of a prominent silversmith. The site includes a working silver shop and pewter foundry. Across Palace Green at the corner of Prince George Street is Wythe House, the home of George Wythe, America's first law professor. Wythe taught Jefferson, Clay, and Marshall. Wythe House served as Washington's headquarters before the seige of Yorktown, and Rochambeau's later. The house, dependencies, and gardens form a miniature plantation layout.

Back on Duke of Gloucester Street, a block east of the Palace is The Magazine, the arsenal of the colony. Authentic arms are exhibited and demonstrated there today.

James Anderson House contains extensive exhibits on Williamsburg archeology and gives visitors a more thorough understanding of what has been accomplished here. And Basset Hall on York Street, southeast of the Capital, is an 18th Century house that served as local residence of Mr. and Mrs. John D. Rockefeller, Jr.

The Bruton Parish Church on Duke of Gloucester Street, just west of Palace Green, is one of America's oldest Episcopal churches. It has been in continuous use since 1715. Nearby is the Public Hospital, the first public institution in the English Colonies devoted exclusively to the treatment of mental illness. The DeWitt Wallace Decorative Arts Gallery, adjoining the Hospital, is a modern museum that features decorative arts of 18th Century America.

TOURS. Tickets to various tours can be bought at the Courthouse of 1770. The carriage ride through the Historic Area is one of the most popular. The 2½-hour Tricorner Hat Tour for children ages 7 to 11 is also popular. The Once Upon a Town Tour is designed for children 4 to 6. The Townsteader Program offers an opportunity for 8 to 14-year-olds to try 18th Century domestic crafts. The Lanthorn Tour offers guided tours of craft shops by candlelight. The Escorted Tour, a 2-hour guided tour through the Historic Area, is the most popular in Williamsburg.

College of William and Mary. Outside the Historic Area, visitors will want to take in the College of William and Mary (1693) at the west end of Duke of Gloucester Street. It is the second oldest college in America, and it initiated the honor system, an elective system of studies, and a school of law and of modern languages. It was the second American institution to have a school of medicine. The Phi Beta Kappa Society was founded here in 1776.

The oldest and most commanding building on the campus is the Wren Building (1695, restored 1928). It is the oldest academic building in America. The Earl Gregg Swem Library, housing the College Museum and Gallery of Colonial Art, and the President's House (1734), the oldest such residence in continuous use in the U.S., are also both on the William and Mary campus.

Also nearby but outside the Historic Area are the Abby Aldrich Rockefeller Folk Art Center (307 S. England St.), which houses American folk painting, sculpture, decorative useful wares, and gardens; and the Craft House, the sales center for approved Williamsburg reproductions. These are located at the Williamsburg Inn and at Merchants Square.

Carter's Grove Plantation is 6 miles southeast of Williamsburg via S. England St. and the "Country Road." The focal point is a 15-room Georgian Mansion (ca. 1750, restored 1927) on a bluff overlooking the James River. It is said that Washington and Jefferson both proposed marriage in this house and were turned down. This is also the site of Wolstenholme Town, an early 17th-Century English Colonial settlement.

STATE PARK. York River State Park has another flavor. Eight miles northwest of Williamsburg on I-64 at the Croaker exit, and north one mile along VA 607 to VA 606E, York River State Park is a 2,491-acre natural preserve along the river and its marshes. It offers fishing, canoe trips, boat launch, hiking trails, picnicking, and nature walks.

THEME PARK. And then there is Busch Gardens— *The Old Country.* Located 3 miles east of Williamsburg on US 60, Busch Gardens is a theme park on 360 acres. The Old Country features an "Oktoberfest" in a re-created German village, plus English, French, Italian, and Scottish villages. Each area has rides, shows, live entertainment, and national restaurants. There is transportation around the grounds by monorail, sky lift, paddleboat, and steam train. Attractions include animal acts, musical reviews, and magic shows, a reproduction of the Globe Theatre, 30 rides (including the super-thrill "Loch Ness Monster" and "da Vinci's Cradle"), arcade, antique carousel, concerts, brewery tour by monorail, miniature of LeMans racetrack, "Rhine River" boat ride, and the "Grimm's Hollow" ride for small children. For further information, call 253-3350.

EXPLORING JAMESTOWN

In mid-May, 1607 a small band of apprehensive English settlers landed on a swampy peninsula near the Bay and founded the first permanent English settlement in the New World. Three small ships, *Susan Constant, Godspeed,* and *Discovery,* brought those first colonists to the place that is Jamestown after landing briefly at Cape Henry near the mouth of the Chesapeake. (The three vessels were re-created and put on display at Jamestown in 1959. *Godspeed* was built again in 1985 after the first replica rotted.)

Jamestown in those early years was anything but an English rose garden. Hostile Indians and voracious mosquitoes plagued the settlers, and there was seldom enough to eat. This was "The Starving Time." Much credit is given to Captain John Smith for holding it all together during those early bad years; if the London Company, patron of the colony, was stubborn but inept, Smith was stubborn and capable. Most historians acknowlege his efforts, for although only a few score settlers survived the first dreadful winter, Jamestown, like Roanoke, North Carolina, might have become another Lost Colony if the remarkable Smith hadn't been there.

But survive it did, and by 1612 Jamestown was producing commercial crops of tobacco, and the colonists were soon producing glass, bricks, and clapboards, fishing nets, pottery, and a variety of implements and tools. The New World's first representative legislative body was established in Jamestown in 1619, only nine years after Lord De la Warre visited the dispirited colonists and persuaded them to hang on. That same year—1619—the first African blacks in the Western Hemisphere arrived aboard a Dutch warship. Like many white new arrivals, they were probably indentured servants who paid for their passage with their labor. Although the English arrived first and established the colony, they were followed in later years by Dutch, French, Scots, Germans, Irish, Welsh, and Italians. Each newcomer brought to the New World a "national" character that would in time be woven into the fabric of Virginia.

When Jamestown became a Royal Colony in 1624, its colonists were already feeling the first stirrings of a new and fierce independence. There was open revolt in 1676 and the village was burned. It was partly rebuilt, but decline was inevitable because of the damp, unhealthy climate. The statehouse was burned in 1698 and the government moved to Williamsburg the following year. By the time of the American Revolution, Jamestown was no longer an active community. At about the same time, the James River eroded the sandy isthmus, and the peninsula became an island.

Nothing of the 17th-Century settlement remains above ground except for the Old Church Tower. However, archaeological exploration by the National Park Service since 1934 has made the outline of the old town clear. Further careful excavation has uncovered foundations, streets, ditches, hedgerows, and fences. Markers, monuments, and recorded messages have been strategically placed to guide Jamestown visitors.

PRACTICAL INFORMATION

FOR JAMESTOWN

HOW TO GET THERE. Jamestown Island in the James River is located about 5 miles southwest of Colonial Williamsburg as the crow flies, approximately 10 miles by car (via Colonial Parkway). Use Rt. 199 off I-64 if you're driving north from Norfolk. There is also a toll ferry from Scotland on the south bank of the James River to Jamestown Festival Park, adjacent to the old town, on Powhatan Creek.

THINGS TO SEE AND DO

TOURING JAMESTOWN. There is a Visitor Center just past the Entrance Station. From there it is possible to walk to all the sights. Starting with "New Towne," the area where Jamestown expanded about 1620, visitors walk along "Back Street" and other original streets. In this area are the sites of Country House and Governor's House, and the homesites of Richard Kemp, (builder of one of the first brick houses in America), Henry Hartwell (a founder of William and Mary), and Dr. John Pott and William Pierce (who led the "thrusting out" of Gov. John Harvey in 1635).

Visitors can also take in the place that has been fixed by tradition as the point on the James that was the First Landing Site. It was also probably the site of the first fort. The Old Church Tower is the only standing ruin of the 17th

Century town. The Tower is believed to be part of the first brick church in America (1636). Memorial Church adjoins the tower. This church was built in 1907 by the Colonial Dames of America over the foundations of the original. Within are foundations said to be those of the earlier church. The foundations of a brick building have also been discovered near the river. These are believed to have been those of the First Statehouse.

There is the Tercentenary Monument near the Jamestown Visitor Center, built in 1907 to commemorate the 300th anniversary of the colony's founding. Other monuments include the Captain John Smith statue, Pocahontas Monument, and Houses of Burgesses Monument (listing members of the first representative legislative body).

There is also a Confederate Fort, built in 1861, near the Old Church Tower. It was one of several Civil War fortifications on the island. Visitors can enjoy a five-mile trail that makes the entire area easily accessible. Finally, visitors can see the Glasshouse, where Colonists first made glass in 1608. There are glass-blowing demonstrations daily.

Jamestown is open to visitors daily from mid-June through Labor Day, 9 to 7; after Labor Day through October and from April till mid-June to 5:30, and November through March till 5. Closed Christmas.

 FESTIVAL PARK. The Jamestown Festival Park area was built in 1957 adjacent to Jamestown to commemorate the 300th birthday of the first permanent English settlement in the New World. Its recreation of early 17th-Century Jamestown includes full-scale replicas of the *Susan Constant, Godspeed,* and *Discovery;* wattle-and-daub buildings in reconstructed James Fort of 1607; and Powhatan's "Indian Village," which has a pottery-making exhibit. The Old World Pavilion presents Virginia's English heritage, while the New World pavilion traces Virginia's history as a colony and later as a state. Both feature audiovisual displays and costumed guides. A Settlement Celebration commemorates the arrival of the first settler each year on May 12.

EXPLORING YORKTOWN

The third treasure of American heritage on the 15-mile wide strip of land known as the Virginia Peninsula is Yorktown. Here, in 1781, American independence was won. Yorktown was first settled in 1630 when free land on the south bank of York was offered those adventurous enough to move out of Jamestown. The Assembly authorized a York River port in 1691 and the town grew quickly, soon becoming a major Colonial shipping center. Its prosperity peaked about 1750 and the port declined when Tidewater Virginia's tobacco trade declined.

Yorktown is most famous as the site of the British surrender in 1781, ending the American Revolution. British commander Cornwallis, after raiding the Virginia countryside almost without resistance, was ordered to establish a port for the winter. The French fleet, lying off the Capes, blocked the British fleet, however, while Washington's troops bottled up the British army on land. The Americans shelled the British from October 9 to October 17, when Cornwallis requested terms. He surrendered two days later while his pipers played "The World Turned Upside Down."

Yorktown today is still an active peninsula community, but many surviving and reconstructed Colonial structures effect an air of 18th Century America. Yorktown Battlefield, the third point of the Colonial National Historical Park, triangle surrounds this Virginia town.

PRACTICAL INFORMATION
FOR YORKTOWN

PLACES TO STAY

MOTELS. Visitors to Yorktown, one of the three major historical sites in Colonial National Historical Park, may very well base themselves in or around Williamsburg, or perhaps across the harbor in Norfolk. Here is a brief list of "local" Yorktown accommodations:

Thomas Nelson Motel. *Moderate.* 2501 George Washington Highway, US 17, 3 miles south of Yorktown; 898–5436. 26 units with kitchenette. Pool.

Tidewater Motel. *Moderate.* Four miles north of Yorktown (over Yorktown Bridge, Rt. 17); 642–2155 or 642–6604. 33 rooms. Pool. Restaurants nearby. Picnic area.

Duke of York. *Moderate.* Water Street on Rt. 238, one block east of the bridge; 898–3232. 57 rooms with balconies. The Duke of York is opposite a beach and overlooks the York river.

Yorktown Motor Lodge. *Inexpensive.* Three and a half miles south of the bridge on US 17; 898–5451. 52 rooms, some with private patios.

HOW TO GET THERE. Yorktown is easily accessible by car from Williamsburg, Newport News, or Norfolk. The Colonial Parkway curves east along the York River from Williamsburg, while I-64, then Rt. 238, comes north from Norfolk, and US 17 crosses the York (north-south) close to town and the battlefield.

TOURIST INFORMATION. First-time visitors to Yorktown should stop first at the modern and spacious Yorktown Victory Center. In one entertaining hour, they will experience the entire spectacle of the Revolutionary War and the decisive victory at Yorktown by George Washington and our French allies over Lord Cornwallis. The Center is open daily year-round (except Christmas), 8:30 to 6, mid-June through Labor Day.

A strikingly realistic film sets the stage for visitors by showing the American Colonies just before the Revolution. A stunning series of multimedia exhibits and artifact displays recreate the sights and sounds of the Revolution from Bunker Hill through Saratoga, Trenton, and Valley Forge, and finally to Yorktown. A dramatic, award-winning film, "The Road to Yorktown," concludes the presentation.

The battlefield itself includes a self-guided tour. The Moore House in which the "articles of capitulation" were drafted is a mile east of the Victory Center on Rt. 238 on the edge of the battlefield. Finally, there is the Yorktown National Civil War Cemetery where more than half the 2,138 buried soldiers are unknown.

THINGS TO SEE AND DO

HISTORIC SITES. In town visitors will discover the **Monument to Alliance and Victory** at the east end of Main Street. It is an elaborately ornamented 95-foot granite column memorializing the American–French alliance in the Revolution.

Swan Tavern at Main and Ballard Sts. is a reconstructed 18th-Century tavern, now an antique shop. The original was destroyed by a gunpowder explosion in 1863. The **York County Courthouse,** across the street from the tavern, was reconstructed in 1955 to resemble the original 1733 courthouse. The town clerk's office has records dating from 1633.

The **Nelson House** at Nelson and Main Sts. is an original restored mansion built by "Scotch Tom" Nelson in the early 1700s. It was the home of his grandson, Thomas Nelson, Jr., one of the signers of the Declaration of Independence. It is an impressive example of Georgian architecture.

Grace Episcopal Church at Church St. was originally built in 1697. It was damaged in 1781, and gutted by fire in 1697. Nevertheless, the original 1649 Communion service is still in use.

SPECIAL INTEREST. Visitors may also want to see the **Virginia Research Center for Archaeology** at the Victory Center. It is conducting one of the most ambitious archaeological projects in North America under the York River, just 3 blocks from the Victory Center. There lies one of General Cornwallis' ships, sunk during the Battle of Yorktown. Ultimately, a specially constructed pier will allow visitors to walk from the shore to watch divers as they carefully excavate the hull and bring its contents to the center. The artifacts will then be placed on exhibit in the **Gallery of the American Revolution** at the Victory Center. The gallery already offers a growing collection that includes the table used by Cornwallis on this southern campaign in America, along with art works and loaned exhibits.

EXPLORING HAMPTON AND
NEWPORT NEWS

Hampton claims to be the oldest English-settled community in the United States. (Jamestown is a park, not a town.) The settlement began in 1610 at a place called Kecoughtan with the building of two stockades as protection against the Kecoughtan Indians. In the late 18th Century, Hamptonians were harassed by pirates until the notorious "Blackbeard" was killed by Captain Henry Maynard. Piracy came to an end here when Blackbeard's crew was jailed in Williamsburg.

Hampton was shelled in the Revolution, burned by the British in the War of 1812, and by its own citizens in 1861 to prevent occupation by the Union. Just five houses survived the last conflagration. Commercial fishing and defense are now the major industries.

Newport News, adjacent to Hampton and closer to Williamsburg, is one of three cities that make up the Port of Hampton Roads. The third is Norfolk. Settled in 1619, Newport News has the world's largest shipbuilding firm, the Newport News Shipbuilding Company, which employs 25,000 workers. Hampton Roads, 14 miles long and 40 feet deep, is formed by the James, York, Elizabeth, and Nansemond Rivers as they pass into the Chesapeake Bay. It is one of the world's finest natural harbors. It sits at the inland end of the historic Virginia Peninsula.

PRACTICAL INFORMATION
FOR HAMPTON AND NEWPORT NEWS

PLACES TO STAY

MOTELS. Visitors to Colonial National Park sometimes find it advantageous to seek accommodations in
Hampton or Newport News. The two cities, across
Hampton Roads from Norfolk are convenient to most of
the peninsula's Colonial sites and are easily accessible from I-64, Norfolk to
Richmond. In general, accommodations in the area may be slightly less expensive than those closer to Colonial Williamsburg or to the south in Norfolk.

Hampton

Holiday Inn. *Moderate.* 1815 W. Mercury Blvd., Exit 8 off I-64; 838–0200.
275 rooms in a 2-story inn. Pool, bar, and room service. Some suites and meeting
rooms. Game room. Golf privileges. Major credit cards.

Chamberlin Hotel. *Moderate.* On the Chesapeake at Fort Monroe; 723–6511
or (800) 582–8975. 210 rooms, with meeting rooms, pools, and sauna. Most
credit cards.

Sheraton Inn–Coliseum. *Moderate.* 1215 W. Mercury Blvd., Exit 8 off I-64;
838–5011. 187 rooms in an 8-story inn. Indoor pool and cafe-bar with entertainment. Meeting rooms. Transportation to terminals. Major credit cards.

Newport News

Holiday Inn. *Expensive.* 6128 Jefferson Ave.; 826–4500. 162 rooms in a
5-story inn. Playground and restaurant. Room service. Bar entertainment.
Major credit cards.

Ramada Inn. *Moderate.* 950 J. Clyde Morris Blvd., Jct. US 17, I-64; 599–
4460. 169 rooms with lighted tennis. 24-hour restaurant. AE, CB, DC, MC, V.

Patton Motel. *Inexpensive.* 1064 Jefferson Ave., 3 miles from I-64; 595–7671.
70 rooms, 30 efficiencies. Pool.

Warwick Motel. *Moderate.* 12304 Warwick Blvd., Rt. 60 at J. Clyde Morris
Blvd.; 599–4444. 31 rooms, with a restaurant. AE, MC, V.

Traveler's Inn. *Inexpensive to Moderate.* 14747 Warwick Blvd.; 838–6852.
105 rooms. Pool and playground. Major credit cards.

Econo Lodge. *Inexpensive.* 15237 Warwick Blvd.; 874–9244. 48 rooms. TV
and sundries. AE, MC, V.

Family Inn. *Inexpensive.* 13700 Warwick Blvd.; 874–4100. 48 rooms. Major
credit cards.

Thr-rift Inn. *Inexpensive.* 6129 Jefferson Ave.; 838–6852. 102 rooms, some with refrigerators. AE, MC, V.

THINGS TO SEE AND DO

Hampton

HISTORIC SITES. In Hampton, **Hampton Monument,** a half mile south on the grounds of the VA Medical Center, marks the approximate spot it is believed the first settlers landed in 1607. **St. John's Church and Parish Museum** on W. Queen's Way and Court St. dates to 1728. Its Bible dates to 1599.

Hampton Institute, east end of Queen St., was founded in 1866 by Union General Samuel Champion, chief of the Freedman's Bureau, to prepare the youth of the South, regardless of color, for the work of organizing school teaching in the South. Many blacks and Indians were educated here. Today, it is Virginia's only coeducational, nondenominational private 4-year college.

SPECIAL-INTEREST TOURS. NASA has a major presence in Virginia; its **Langley Research Center** is 3 miles north of Hampton on VA 134. It offers a self-guided tour of the history of flight, aeronautics research, and space exploration. Space artifacts include moon rock, the Apollo Command Module, and a space suit worn on the moon.

The Big Bethel Battlefield commemorates the first "regular" battle of the Civil War. The Sums-Eaton Museum at 418 W. Mercury Blvd. exhibits Hampton's history. The **Kecoughtan Indian Village** at 418 W. Mercury Blvd. is a reproduction of an early Indian village. **Bluebird Gap Farm** at 60 Pine Chapel Rd. is a 15-acre farm with a barnyard zoo; indigenous wildlife including black bears, deer, wolves; and antique and modern farm equipment. It offers picnic and playgrounds. **Aerospace Park** at 413 Mercury Blvd., has jet aircraft and missile exhibits. (Open daily.) **Fort Monroe,** 3 miles southeast of Hampton, near I-64, stands on the site of a 1609 stockade. The **Casemate Museum** is at the fort, which was completed about 1834.

BEACHES. Buckroe Beach on Rt. 351 offers swimming, boating, and fishing on the Chesapeake Bay. It has a 12-acre amusement park.

Newport News

MUSEUMS. The premier attraction in Newport News is the **Mariners Museum** at the junction of US 60 and Clyde Morris Blvd. (595–0368). It features a collection of international scope devoted to maritime history in the broadest sense, including inland navigation. Exhibits include the Hall of Steamships, Chesapeake Bay Gallery, Gibbs Gallery, small craft, ships' carvings, ship models, Crabtree Collection of Miniature Ships, marine decorative arts, marine paintings, seapower, and temporary special exhibits. There is a research library and a 550-acre park with a 167-acre fishing lake and picnic area.

Since the beginning of time, the sea has captured the imagination of men. The many who were inspired to explore her waters could not have done so were it not for the craftsmen who built their vessels. It is to these craftsmen that the Mariners Museum is dedicated.

The War Memorial Museum of Virginia at 9285 Warwick Blvd. offers a comprehensive display of more than 30,000 artifacts, including weapons, uniforms, vehicles, posters, insignia, and accoutrements relating to every major American military involvement from the Revolution to Vietnam.

HARBOR CRUISE. *Wharton's Wharf Harbor Cruise* aboard the *American Patriot* leaves the boat harbor, south end of Jefferson Ave. at 12th street for a 2-hour narrated cruise on Hampton Roads, the world's largest natural harbor. Also Intercoastal Waterway and evening cruises. Call 245–1533 for prices and schedules.

OTHER ATTRACTIONS. Peninsula Nature and Science Center at 524 J. Clyde Morris Blvd., in Deer Park, offers exhibits on natural science. Open daily; call 599–6800. Fort Eustis on Mulberry Island (northwest end of the city on James River) is the headquarters of the U.S. Army Transportation Center, and includes a miniature Army port and the *Army Transportation Museum* depicting the development of army transportation from 1776 to the present. Open daily except Jan. 1 and Christmas. Call 878–5787. The **Peninsula Fine Arts Center** on Museum Drive exhibits the Tidewater's and Virginia's artists and craftsmen. Closed Monday and holidays. Call 596–8175. Free.

PARK. Newport News Park, more than 8,000 acres located a mile north of Rts. 105 and 143, has canoes, paddleboats, and rental boats, nature trails and rental bikes, freshwater fishing and golf, and supervised camp sites. Open year-round. Call 877–5381 for park information, or Virginia Peninsula Tourism Council, 838–4184 for general area information.

EXPLORING JAMES RIVER PLANTATIONS

Historic plantations dot the banks of the James River from Williamsburg to Richmond. Three of the most important along Rt. 5 begin with **Sherwood Forest,** 20 miles from Williamsburg, the plantation home of John Tyler, tenth President of the United States. It was also owned by William Henry Harrison, the ninth President. This is the longest frame house in America, the same length as a football field. Still in the Tyler family, it includes magnificent furnishings and stands on 12 acres of grounds with 80 varieties of trees. Sherwood Forest dates from 1730.

Berkeley, three miles from Shirley (below), has no peer among the James River plantations as a center of historic interest. It is a beautifully restored example of the mansions that graced Virginia's "Golden Age." This was the site of what Virginians say was the first official Thanksgiving in 1619. It was also the birthplace of Benjamin Harrison, a signer of the Declaration of Independence, and William Henry Harrison, the ninth President. It was the ancestral home of President Benjamin Harrison and the headquarters for General McClellan. "Taps" was written there in 1862. It was built in 1726, and today it is in outstanding condition with exceptionally fine period antiques.

Finally, **Shirley** (1723), 20 miles from Richmond, has no rival in Queen Anne architectural style. A complete set of 18th Century brick buildings form a Queen Anne forecourt, unique in this country. The mansion, on the banks of the James River, has been the home of the Carters since 1723. The original family portraits, silver, furnishing, superb paneling, and carved walnut staircase are there to see. Shirley was the Home of Anne Hill Carter, mother of Robert E. Lee, and is owned and operated by the ninth generation of Carters.

Plantations that may be visited by the public are well marked along Rt. 5, a pleasant 51-mile drive along the James River between Williamsburg and Richmond. For information, fees, and visiting times, phone Sherwood Forest (829–5377) or Shirley (795–2385). There are fees for these and other plantation tours.

Amy
Harold

VIRGINIA'S NORTHERN NECK

Surrounded by natural waterways and laced with creeks and inlets, Virginia's Northern Neck is a boating and fishing paradise. Wherever you go on the Neck, visitors are never far from a marina or a boat landing. You can sail the Bay and the rivers, spend a day cruising in a powerboat, paddle a canoe on quiet ponds or creeks, or engage one of the friendly and experienced charter tour boat captains for a day of saltwater excitement. Northern Neck explorers shouldn't miss the daily guided cruises to historic Tangier and Smith Islands.

At the end of the day, there is nothing better than a Northern Neck seafood feast. Visitors will find fresh fish, crabs, and oysters served everywhere on the Neck, along with vegetables from local gardens and hush puppies. It is all part of the "Chesapeake Bay Lifestyle."

Peace and quiet are the Northern Neck's most precious assets, but there is also plenty to see and do. Visitors can loosen up with golf or tennis or unwind on secluded campsites or peaceful nature trails. Water skiing, swimming, and wind-surfing are all at their doorsteps.

146

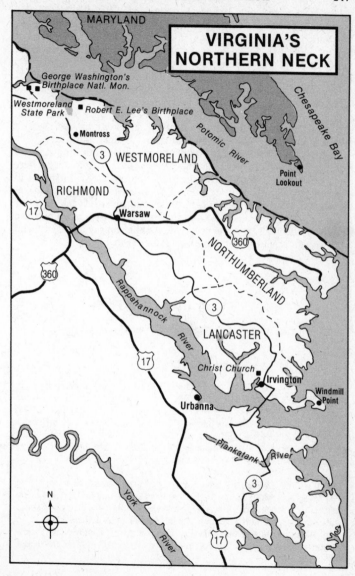

VIRGINIA'S NORTHERN NECK

The Neck is also rich with the early history of the Republic. At the upper end of the Neck, visitors can find the birthplace of George Washington and the ancestral home of the rich and powerful Lee family of Virginia. At the lower end are historic Christ Church and the tomb of Robert "King" Carter of Carter's Grove outside Williamsburg. In between are working plantations, Colonial churches, and quaint villages dating back 300 years. Just reading historic markers can take a full day in the Neck.

And if visitors are captivated by the past, there is no need to break the spell at the end of the day. Fine resorts, historic inns, and pleasant motels offer gracious hospitality that many thought had died.

History, relaxation, fishing and boating, and gracious dining are all a part of the Northern Neck, but they do not tell the whole story. There is something more to the area, something that makes visitors want to come back again and again. It is the charm of everyday country life and the lure of town market days and bustling country fairs. It is local crafts and music. It is seafood fresh from the boat and crisp garden produce fresh from the fields. It is the people who smile and say hello, and who want to help make the most of each visitor's stay.

PRACTICAL INFORMATION
FOR VIRGINIA'S NORTHERN NECK

WHERE TO STAY

HOTELS AND MOTELS. Virginia's Northern Neck, lying south of the Potomac River, is "country"—quiet towns, quiet farmlands, quiet river and Bay-front coves. Like neighboring Maryland counties on the north bank of the river, the Neck's small towns and villages boast only few really notable accommodations. However, Williamsburg and Norfolk are but a few hours drive to the south, via US 17, and Richmond is even closer to the southwest (US 360).

The Tides Inn. *Deluxe.* Located a quarter of a mile south of Irvington on Rt. 3; 438–5000 or (800) 446–9981. 109 rooms in an inn that belies our opening statement. Golf lodge. Private beach, paddleboats, sailboats, canoes, and yacht cruises. Private patios and balconies. The inn is situated on 25 landscaped acres on a hill and is surrounded on 3 sides by water. Bar and a notable New Orleans restaurant, Cap'n B's, which has a plantation ambience. MC, V for both inn and restaurants.

The Tides Lodge. *Expensive.* Irvington; 438–6000 or (800) 446–5660. 60 rooms, with golf course, tennis, yacht cruises, and heated pool. Luxury in a rural setting. Major credit cards.

Whispering Pines. *Moderate.* Located 2 miles east of Irvington on Rt. 200; 435–1101. 29 rooms with golf privileges and picnic tables on wooded grounds. Restaurant near. MC, V.

Windmill Point Marine Resort. *Moderate.* Located 9½ miles southeast of Irvington (Rt. 695); 435–1166. 42 rooms with private patios and balconies, marina with slips, and golf privileges. Bar and pool. Most major credit cards.

Washington and Lee Motel, *Inexpensive.* Located one mile south of Montross on Rt. 3; 493–8093. 39 rooms. Cafe nearby. MC, V.

PLACES TO EAT

RESTAURANTS. Although our selection of restaurants in the Northern Neck area is not extensive, we are open to suggestions. Seafood, especially crab, is stressed here—and who could ask for anything more? Prices in general reflect the area's rural atmosphere; this is back-country Bay-side, not Norfolk or Richmond or Virginia Beach.

Pete Allen Oyster Company and Seafood. *Inexpensive.* Route 1, Montrose; 493–8711. Although this is a carry-out only, it's worth the effort; here is crab cookery at its best. Pete Allen's crab cakes are a delight. Open year round, longer hours during the crab season.

Pearson's Seafood. *Inexpensive.* 610 Colonial Ave., Colonial Beach; 224–7511. Live, steamed, and softshelled crabs. Open April to November. Carry-out only. Open to 6 P.M.

Northern Neck Seafood. *Inexpensive.* Located on US 360, Red Hill, Warsaw. Open all year, this carry-out (only) offers steamed crabs, softshelled crabs, or—in fact—crabs just about any way you want them. Eight in the morning till 8 at night. Beer.

THINGS TO SEE AND DO

HOW TO GET THERE. Northern Neck is made up of four rural counties: Lancaster, Richmond, Northumberland, and Westmoreland. The area can be reached via US 360, northeast from Richmond, or US 17, north from Newport News or south from Fredericksburg. Rt. 3 crosses the Rappahannock River from Middlesex County into Lancaster near the Bay, then threads its way northwest up the middle of the Neck.

Lancaster County

Lancaster County, which was formed in 1651, is a blend of saltwater vitality with venerable Colonial history. Site of numerous outstanding marinas, quiet coves and anchorages, and beautiful scenery along the Rappahannock and Chesapeake shores, Lancaster County is "Chesapeake Bay Living" at its best.

Windmill Point. Located on the southeastern tip of Northern Neck, Windmill Point offers a spectacular view of the Rappahannock, where the river joins the Bay. Nearby between White Stone and Kilmarnock is Christ Church, which has been described as "the most perfect example of Colonial church architecture now remaining in Virginia." It was completed in 1732 as a gift from Robert "King" Carter of nearby Corotoman. The **Merry Point Ferry,** one of the few remaining river ferries in Virginia, offers a delightful free crossing of scenic Corotoman River.

Lancaster Courthouse. The county seat since 1742, the town of Lancaster offers a trip into the past of early Tidewater Virginia. Around Court House Green are the original clerk's office (1797), Colonial jail, and Courthouse (1863). **Mary Ball Washington Museum and Library** is located in Lancaster House, also on Court House Green.

Epping Forest, built about 1690, was the birthplace of Mary Ball, the mother of George Washington.

Northumberland County

Northumberland is known as the "Mother County" of the Northern Neck because several Virginia counties were carved from its original land. First settled in 1635 and officially formed in 1648, the county is bordered by the wide Potomac and sparkling Chesapeake Bay, blending recreational opportunities with the quiet, historic atmosphere for which the Neck is famous.

Reedville. Located near the northern tip of the Neck, Reedville is one of the busiest fishing Bay ports in Virginia. The village provides a living image of the past with its magnificent Victorian mansions and seafaring atmosphere. Accessible by regularly scheduled boat cruises from Reedville, Smith and Tangier Islands are quaint and historic. Their residents depend upon the Chesapeake completely for their livelihood.

Chesapeake Bay and the Potomac provide excellent fishing and crabbing as well as 438 miles of shoreline (including inland waterways). Public boat ramps are available throughout the county. Other attractions include charter fishing, marinas, and campgrounds. The fresh seafood available at local oyster and crab houses enhances any visit.

Sunnybank Ferry. The Ferry at Sunnybank offers free crossing for vehicles over the beautiful Little Wicomico River, and *Heathville,* Northumberland's picturesque county seat, provides historic attractions including the **County Courthouse, Ball Memorial Library and Museum,** and **St. Stephens Church.**

Richmond County

Richmond County was formed in 1692 and named for the reigning favorite at the Court of William and Mary. The county stretches along the beautiful and unspoiled Rappahannock River. *Warsaw,* the county seat since 1730, was originally called Richmond County Courthouse. The village was renamed in 1831 in sympathy with the Polish struggle for liberty. Warsaw is the site of the **Courthouse** and **Clerk's Office**, built in 1816. The town is a commercial center, with a variety of shops and is the home of the North Campus of **Rappahannock Community College.**

North Farnham Church. Built in the form of a Latin cross, North Farnham Church is a beautiful example of Colonial architecture. Naylors, located beside an attractive Rappahannock River beach, was the seat of Richmond County's government from 1692 to 1730. The Rappahannock River offers beaches, crabbing, fishing, and water sports, plus lovely, peaceful countryside stretching back from the river's edge.

Westmoreland County

Westmoreland County, named for a British shire, was founded in 1652 by the Colonial government in Jamestown. The birthplace or home of more statesmen of national stature than any other county in the country, Westmoreland produced such leaders as George Washington, James Monroe, and Robert E. Lee.

Washington's Birthplace National Monument. Located in Wakefield, this is the site of our first President's birth. Wakefield provides a wealth of insight into life on an 18th-Century plantation. Of special interest are the Visitor's Center, a memorial house of 18th-Century design, a Colonial working farm, and the family burial plot.

Stratford Hall. Perhaps the most majestic of the Colonial plantations in Virginia, Stratford Hall was the ancestral home of the Lee family, and the birthplace of two signers of the Declaration of Independence and Robert E. Lee. Built in the 1720s, the restored mansion is furnished with exquisite period pieces. The 1,600-acre plantation includes gardens, stable, a working gristmill, and cliffs overlooking the Potomac.

The Historic Courthouse Area in Montross features the old courthouse (ca. 1707), standing on the site of the original courthouse (ca. 1667), and the *Westmoreland Museum.* **Colonial Beach** on the Potomac has been a popular river resort for more than a century. The town sponsors the **Potomac River Festival** and an outdoor art festival.

Westmoreland State Park. The park, also on the Potomac, offers cabins, camping, picnic areas, hiking, a public boat ramp, and swimming at the beach or in a new Olympic-size swimming pool.

This visit to Virginia's Northern neck completes this guidebook's clockwise tour around Chesapeake Bay, for just to the north, across the Potomac, are Maryland's Calvert, Charles, and St. Mary's Counties, back where we began.

Speak a foreign language in seconds.

Now an amazing space age device makes it possible to speak a foreign language *without* having to learn a foreign language.

Speak French, German, or Spanish.
With the incredible Translator 8000—world's first pocket-size electronic translation machines —you're never at a loss for words in France, Germany, or Spain.

8,000-word brain.
Just punch in the foreign word or phrase, and English appears on the LED display. Or punch in English, and read the foreign equivalent instantly.

Only 4¾" x 2¾", it possesses a fluent 8,000-word vocabulary (4,000 English, 4,000 foreign). A memory key stores up to 16 words; a practice key randomly calls up words for study, self-testing, or game use. And it's also a full-function calculator.

150,000 sold in 18 months.
Manufactured for Langenscheidt by Sharp/Japan, the Translator 8000 comes with a 6-month warranty. It's a valuable aid for business and pleasure travelers, and students. It comes in a handsome leatherette case, and makes a super gift.

Order now with the information below.

INDEX

INDEX

Aberdeen Proving Ground, 72, 73, 77

Accomack (VA), 105–107

Accomack County, 105

Air, arrival by, 13

American Revolution, 4, 31, 41, 53, 73, 77, 90, 118

AMTRAK service, 13

Amusement parks, 101, 102, 121, 127, 130, 135–136, 143

Anderson, James, 134

Annapolis (MD), 4, 6, 13, 43, 51–58
  boat trips from, 27, 57
  hotels and motels in, 55–56
  map of, 52
  restaurants in, 56–57
  things to see and do in, 23, 25, 54–55, 57–58

Anne Arundel County, 13, 23, 53

Antique automobiles, 23

Antique shows, 23, 25, 45

Antiques, shopping for, 68, 78, 102, 140

Apollo Command Module, 143

Aquarium, 69

Archaeology research center, 140–141

Art, 23, 24, 50, 68, 112, 121. *See also* Museums—art

Assateague Island, 7, 24, 96–97, 105, 108–109

Association for Research and Enlightenment, 121

Aviation Day, 25

Bach Festival, 24

Back River, 2

Ballet, 121

Baltimore, Lords (the Calverts), 4, 40, 51–53, 91

Baltimore (MD), 2, 13, 59–69
  Battle of, 25
  boat trips from, 27, 68–69
  calendar of, 23–26
  hotels and motels in, 62–63
  map of, 60
  nightlife of, 69
  restaurants in, 63–65
  things to see and do in, 61, 65–69
  water taxi at, 66

Baltimore County, 13, 72

Barbershop quartets, 23

Baseball, 67, 68, 120

Basilica of the Assumption of the Blessed Virgin Mary, 66

Beaches, 96, 100–101, 112, 120–121, 143

Bed and breakfast establishments, 73, 85, 86, 116

Berkeley (home), 33, 145

Big Bethel Battlefield, 143

Birdwatching, 108

Black Hawk, 32

Blackbeard the Pirate, 103, 141

Blacks, first African, 136

Boat-launching ramps, 28

Boat races, 24

Boat rides, 5, 27–28, 50, 57, 76, 91, 122, 144, 150. *See also* Yacht chartering

Boat shows, 6, 23–25

Boatbuilding. *See* Shipbuilding

Boating, 11, 57, 65, 76, 88, 122

Bohemia River, 3

Booth, John Wilkes, 49

Bridges, 42

British visitors, 15

Bruton Parish Church, 129, 134

Bus travel, 13

Busch Gardens, 127, 130, 135–136

Byrd, William, II, 33

Calendars of events, 22–26, 45

Calvert County, 47–49

Cambridge (MD), 6, 24, 25, 85, 87, 90

Campgrounds, 28–29, 83, 116–117

Canals, 72, 77

Canoeing, 29, 83, 105, 144

Cape Charles, 106–107, 109

Cape Henry, 120

Caroline County, 83, 85, 87, 88, 91

Carroll, Charles, 66

Carter, George, 33

Carter, Robert "King," 148, 150

Carter's Grove, 129, 135

Cayce, Edgar, 121

Cecil County, 13, 72–75

Centreville (MD), 81, 88

Champion, Samuel, 143

Charles I (king of England), 40

Charles County, 47–50

Charlestown (MD), 77

Chesapeake Bay, map of, viii–ix

Chesapeake Bay Bridge–Tunnel, 42, 105, 106

Chesapeake City (MD), 24, 73, 77

Chester River, 3

Chestertown (MD), 74

Children, accommodations for, 20

Children's festivals, 23

Chincoteague (VA), 7, 23–26, 105, 107, 108

Choptank River, 3, 25, 83, 90–92

Churches and cathedrals
    Maryland, 66, 83, 89, 90, 92
    Virginia, 107, 110, 127, 134, 137–139, 140, 143, 150, 151

Civil War, 4, 24–25, 31, 41, 53, 61, 90, 138, 140, 141, 143, 145
    memorial days for, 22, 24
    museum of, 50.
    See also Lincoln, Abraham

Claiborne, William, 40, 44–45, 81

Clams, 107

Clay, Henry, 134

Climate, 11, 42–43

College of William and Mary, 32, 125, 129, 135

Colleges, renting dormitory rooms at, 16–17

Colonial Beach (VA), 24

Colonial Dames of America, 138

Colonial National Historical Park, map of, 128

Colonial sites, 31–34, 50, 66, 77, 90, 91, 102, 106–107, 121.
    See also Jamestown; Williamsburg; Yorktown

Constellation, U.S.S., 4, 66,

Coode, John, 40

Cornwallis, Lord, 32, 139

Cost of trip, 16–18

County fairs, 23, 24

Courthouses, 49, 88, 89, 106, 121, 138, 140, 150, 151

Cousteau Oceans Center, 112
Crabbing, 92, 150
Crisfield (MD), 24, 25, 84, 86–88, 91, 92, 109
Customs House, 89
Cypress, 24, 49

Davis, Jefferson, 32
Davis, Westmoreland, 33
De la Warr, Baron (Thomas West), 39–40, 136
Deal Island, 84, 91
Delmarva Peninsula, 7, 23–25
Deltaville (VA), 7–8
Denton (MD), 85, 87, 91
Disabled travelers, tips for, 15
Dismal Swamp, 119
Dog show, 25
Dorchester County, 13, 25, 83, 85, 87–90
Dormitory rooms, renting, 16–17
Dos Passos, John, 66

East New Market (MD), 90
Eastern River, 3
Eastern Shore, 6–7, 13–14, 80–93, 103–110
  boat trips from, 27, 88
  hotels and motels on, 84–86, 109–110
  maps of, 82, 104
  restaurants on, 86–87, 110
  rivers of, 3
  things to see and do on, 88–93, 106–109
Easton (MD), 24, 26, 81, 84, 85, 87
Eastville (VA), 103, 106
Edgewater (MD), 25
Elizabeth I (queen of England), 5

Elizabeth River, 111, 141
Elkton (MD), 72
Epping Forest, 150
Eyre Hall, 106

Fell, William, 61
Ferry rides. See Boat rides
Fishing
  freshwater, 29, 78, 83, 92, 120, 135
  ocean, 28, 29, 102, 105, 112, 120, 122, 150
  show of, 22
  tournaments of, 24, 29, 112
Flower displays, 23, 24, 118
Football, 68
Forts, 4, 32, 41, 50, 66, 81, 127, 138, 143
Fossil scavenging, 49
4-wheel-drive races, 25

Gardens, 77, 89, 118
Geddy, James, 134
Glass, 119, 138
Golfing, 122
Goodwin, W. A. R., 129
Grant, U. S., 2
Gunpowder River, 2

Halloween festivals, 25, 26
Hampton (VA), 32, 127, 141–143
Hampton Institute, 143
Hampton Roads, Port of, 141, 144
Handy, Isaac, 91
Harford County, 13, 72–77
Harrison, Benjamin, 33, 145
Harrison, William Henry, 144, 145
Hartwell, Henry, 137
Harvey, John, 137

Harve de Grace (MD), 22, 23, 25, 76, 77
Heartville (VA), 150
Henrietta Maria (queen of England), 4, 40
Henry, Marguerite, 108
Henry, Patrick, 33, 127, 129, 134
Hicks, Thomas Holliday, 90
Highways. *See* Motorists, tips for
History, 1–2, 4–5, 37–41. *See also* specific places and wars
Hockey, 68
Hooper's Island (MD), 24
Horse and carriage show, 23
Horse races, 24, 68, 72
Hotels and motels, 16–20. *See also* specific places
Hunting of deer and quail, 93. *See also* Wildfowl
Hydroplane races, 25

Ice skating, 76
Indians, 25, 26, 32, 38, 40, 41, 83, 90, 136, 141, 143
Iron furnace, 102

James River, 2, 3, 32, 125, 137, 141
  plantations of, 144–145
Jamestown, 3, 5, 23, 32, 39–40, 105, 124, 127, 136–138
  map of, 128
  things to see and do in, 137–138
Jefferson, Thomas, 127, 129, 134, 135
Jones, John Paul, 57

Kecoughtan (VA), 141
Kemp, Richard, 137
Kent County, 13, 73–76
Kent Island (MD), 40, 44, 81
Key, Francis Scott, 4

Lacrosse, 68
Lancaster County, 149–150
Lee, Light Horse Harry, 33
Lee, Robert E., 8, 33, 145, 151
Lighthouses, 49, 76, 109, 121
Lincoln, Abraham, 2, 49
Liquor, 18

MacArthur, Douglas, 119
Madison, James, 33
Magothy River, 2
Mardela Springs, 91
Marshall, John, 134
Maryland
  facts on, 4–5
  shores of, 2–3
  tourist information for, 13–14, 22, 58.
  See also specific areas
Mason-Dixon Line, 91
Maynard, Henry, 141
Maypole dance, 23
McClellan, George B., 145
McCrea, Mr. and Mrs. Archibald, 129
Mencken, H.L., 66
Mental hospital, first American, 134
Michener, James, 83
Mills, 50, 76, 90
Monitor vs. *Merrimac*, 41
Monroe, James, 33, 151
Morven Park, 33
Mosquitoes, 43, 136
Motels. *See* Hotels and motels

Motorists, tips for, 12–14, 76, 88, 94–96, 137, 139, 149
Mudd, Samuel A., 49
Museums, 67–68, 119, 121
  archaeological, 49
  Army transportation, 144
  art, 67, 68, 119, 134, 135, 144
  baseball, 67
  canal, 77
  Civil War, 50
  farm, 90, 143
  glass, 119
  history, 50, 67, 78, 89, 92, 101, 102, 119, 143, 150, 151
  hunting and fishing, 77
  Indian, 90
  industrial, 67
  Life Saving Station, 101
  maritime, 32, 49, 67, 68, 89, 90, 121, 122, 125, 143–144
  natural science, 144
  nuclear, 49
  oceanic, 112
  Oriental, 32, 119
  railway, 49
  of rural life, 23, 77, 92
  science, 67
  space, 143
  tobacco, 49–50
  war and weapons, 77, 144
  War of 1812, 66
  wax, 121
  wildfowl art, 91
Music, 24, 66, 67, 112, 119, 121
Myers, Moses, 32, 118

Nansemond River, 141
Nanticoke River, 3, 92
NASA, 108–109, 143
NATO, 111

Natural history areas, 28, 50, 76, 78
Necks, definition of, 81
Needlework show, 25
Nelson, Thomas, Jr., 140
Nettles, 26, 43
Newport News (VA), 32, 41, 141–144
Norfolk (VA), 7, 23, 24, 26, 111–114, 116–120
  boat trips from, 28, 120
  hotels and motels in, 114
  map of, 113
  restaurants in, 117
  things to see and do in, 32, 112, 118–120
North Farnham Church, 151
Northampton County, 105
Northern Neck, 8, 125, 146–151
  hotels and motels in, 148–149
  map of, 147
  restaurants in, 149
  things to see and do in, 149–151
Northumberland County, 150
Nuclear plant and museum, 42, 49

Oatlands Plantation, 33
Ocean City (MD), 7, 23, 94–102
  boat trips from, 27–28, 101
  hotels and motels in, 97–99
  restaurants in, 99–100
  things to see and do in, 100–102
Onancock (VA), 24, 107
Opera, 119
Oxford (MD), 6, 85
Oyster (VA), 7, 107
Oyster boats, 4, 49, 66, 84, 89, 91
Oysters, 7, 25, 26, 45, 107, 108

Parks and forests, 28–29, 49, 50, 76–78, 83, 96, 102, 120, 135, 144, 151.
  See also Wildlife refuges
Patrapsco River, 2
Patuxet River, 2, 25, 45, 49, 50
Penn, William, 89, 91
Phi Beta Kappa Society, 135
Philadelphia (PA), 2
Piankatank River, 3, 7
Pickersgill, Mary, 66
Pierce, William, 137
Piracy, 103, 141
Plantations, 33, 50, 77, 125, 129, 134, 144–145, 148
Pocahontas, 40, 138
Poe, Edgar Allan, 66
Pokomoke City (MD), 24
Ponies. *See* Wild ponies
Portsmouth (VA), 24, 25, 125
  boat trips from, 28
Potomac River, 2, 8, 25, 150, 151
Pott, John, 137
Powhatan, Chief, 40, 125, 138
Princess Anne (MD), 84, 86, 87, 92

Quaker meeting house, 89
Queen Anne's County, 13, 81, 84, 86, 88–89

Rail travel, 13
Raleigh, Sir Walter, 39
Rappahannock River, 3, 8, 150–151
Reading material, 16
Reedville (VA), 88, 109, 150
Religious toleration, 4, 40
Restaurants, 20–22.
  See also specific areas
Richmond County, 150–151

Roanoke, 39, 136
Rochambeau, Comte de, 134
Rock Hall (MD), 78
Rockefeller, John D., Jr., 129, 134
Rolfe, John, 40, 125

St. Clement's Island, 25, 44–45, 50
St. John's College, 53, 54
St. Leonard's Creek, Battle of, 49
St. Mary's City (MD), 24, 25, 45, 50
St. Mary's County, 13, 47–50
St. Michaels (MD), 25, 81, 85–87, 89
Salisbury (MD), 83, 85–87, 91
Sassafras River, 3, 77, 78
Scuba, 122
Seafood, 3–4
Senior citizen discounts, 18
Severn River, 2, 53
Sherwood Forest (plantation), 33, 144–145
Shipbuilding, 8, 141
Shirley Plantation, 33, 145
Shot tower, 66
Skiing, 76
Smith, John, 11, 32, 40–44, 49, 72, 84, 105, 109, 136, 138
Smith Island, 84, 86, 88, 92, 109, 150
Snorkeling, 122
Snow Hill (MD), 102
Soccer, 68
Soda fountain, 101
Somerset County, 13, 84, 86–88, 91–92
South River, 2
Sportfishing. *See* Fishing
Stamp Act, 106

"Star-Spangled Banner," 4, 66
Stratford Hall, 33, 151
Strawberry Festival, 24
Street cars, 23, 65, 122
Surfboarding, 101
Susquehanna River, 2, 25, 37–38, 77
Swimming, 26

Talbot County, 13, 81–83, 86–89
Tall ships, 24, 68, 112
Tangier Island, 88, 105, 109, 150
"Taps," 145
Taylor's Island, 89–90
Telephone, 16
Tennis, 122
Thanksgiving, first, 125
Theater, 24, 79, 101, 106, 107, 119
Thoroughgood, Adam, 32
Tides, 3
Tidewater Virginia, 124–145
  map of, 126.
  See also Jamestown;
    Williamsburg; Yorktown
Tilghman Island, 89
Time zone, 16
Tipping, 21
Tobacco, 45, 49–50, 136, 138
Tourist homes, 16
Tourist information. See under
  specific state
Tred Avon River, 3, 89
Trolley cars. See Street cars
Turtle Derby, 24
Tyler, John, 33, 144–145

United States Navy
  Monitor, victory of, 41
  mothballed fleet of, 7
    Naval Academy, 6, 24, 53, 54, 57–58
    Norfolk Naval Station, 119
    Oceana Naval Air Station, 121
Upper Bay, 70–79
  hotels and motels of, 73–74
  map of, 71
  restaurants of, 74–76
  things to see and do in, 76–79
Urbanna (VA), 8, 26

Verranzano, Giovanni de, 39
Vienna (MD), 85, 90
Virginia
  facts about, 5
  tourist information for, 14, 22, 120, 122.
  See also Northern Neck;
    Tidewater Virginia
Virginia Beach (VA), 23–25, 112–113, 115–118, 120–123
  boat rides from, 122
  hotels and motels in, 115–116
  map of, 113
  restaurants in, 118
  things to see and do in, 120–123

Wachapreague (VA), 7, 24
Wakefield (Washington's home), 33, 151
Wallops launch site, 108–109
War of 1812, 4, 25, 41, 49, 66, 89–90, 141
Ward, Steve and Lem, 92
Warsaw (VA), 150–151
Washington, George, 4, 32, 33, 53, 66, 78, 119, 125, 135, 148, 151
  at Yorktown, 134, 139
Washington, Mary Ball, 150

Washington College, 78
Water pollution, 4
Waterfowl. *See* Wildfowl
Weather, 11, 42–43
West River, 2
Western Shore, 7–8, 13, 44–50
   boat trips from, 3, 27, 88
   hotels and motels in, 47–48
   map of, 46
   restaurants in, 48
   rivers of, 2–3
   things to see and do in, 49–50
Westmoreland County, 151
Whitehaven (MD), 91
Wicomico County, 13, 83,
   85–88, 91
Wicomico River, 3, 91, 92, 150
Wild ponies, 7, 24, 96, 97, 105,
   108
Wildfowl, 23, 26, 43, 78, 83, 90,
   93, 108
Wildlife refuges, 78, 83, 90, 105,
   108, 119, 120
Williamsburg, 32, 125, 127–137
   hotels and motels in and
     around, 130–132

   map of, 128
   restaurants in and around,
     132–133
   things to see and do in and
     around, 133–136
Wilson, Woodrow, 33
Wolstenholme Towne, 130, 135
Women, first Maryland votes
   by, 78
Worcester County, 94–102
   map of, 95
Wye Oak, 81, 89
Wythe, George, 134

Yacht chartering, 30–31, 57,
   120
York River, 3, 138, 141
Yorktown, 32, 41, 138–141
   map of, 128
   motels in, 139
   things to see and do in,
     140–141
Youth hostel, 63

Zoos, 69, 91, 119, 143